Ernst Kasper – Bauten und Projekte 1965 – 2005

Deutsches Architektur Museum – Aktuelle Galerie
27. August bis 25. September 2005

Ernst Kasper – Buildings and Projects 1965 – 2005

Deutsches Architektur Museum – Aktuelle Galerie
27 August through 25 September, 2005

 DEUTSCHES ARCHITEKTUR MUSEUM

DAM – Deutsches Architektur Museum – Aktuelle Galerie

Konzeption der Aktuellen Galerie des DAM
Ingeborg Flagge

Kuratorin der Ausstellung und Herausgeberin des Katalogs
Susanne Gross, Köln

Redaktion
Ingrid van Hüllen, Aachen
Carsten Krettek, Aachen

Übersetzungen
Jeremy Gaines, Frankfurt am Main

Lektorat
Hannah Ostfeld, Köln

Gestaltung
Studio Joachim Mildner, Düsseldorf
Layout
Sandra Hagedorn

© DAM 2005

ISBN 3-9808887-9-7

DAM – Deutsches Architektur Museum – Aktuelle Galerie

Concept for Aktuelle Galerie of the DAM
Ingeborg Flagge

Curator of the exhibition and catalogue editing
Susanne Gross, Cologne

Editorial
Ingrid van Hüllen, Aachen
Carsten Krettek, Aachen

Translation
Jeremy Gaines, Frankfurt on Main

Copyreading
Hannah Ostfeld, Cologne

Graphic Design
Studio Joachim Mildner, Düsseldorf
Layout
Sandra Hagedorn

© DAM 2005

ISBN 3-9808887-9-7

Inhalt

Projekte

Content

Projects

Ingeborg Flagge
Vorwort

Die Aktuelle Galerie des Deutschen Architektur Museums zeigt anlässlich des 70. Geburtstages von Ernst Kasper die erste monographische Ausstellung zu seinem Werk. Ernst Kasper war Professor an der Kunstakademie Düsseldorf, wo er 28 Jahre lehrte. Ganze Architektengenerationen haben ihn gefürchtet und verehrt und sind von ihm geprägt worden. Bis heute führt Ernst Kasper sein eigenes Architekturbüro in Aachen. Ernst Kasper und seine Architektur waren und sind bis heute ein Geheimtipp: Sein Werk ist erst noch zu entdecken. Das liegt daran, dass Kasper in einer Welt der publikationsgierigen Baumeister die absolute Ausnahme war und ist. Leise, aber bestimmt ist er seinen Weg gegangen – und zahlreiche erste Preise bezeugen, dass die außergewöhnliche Qualität seiner Entwürfe verstanden wurde.

Die Ausstellung im DAM thematisiert zwei Bereiche:
Sie zeigt Kaspers ausgeführte Bauten, hier an prominentester Stelle das Kaiserbad-Gelände in Aachen, ein fulminantes Beispiel der ganz besonderen Fähigkeit des Architekten, die speziellen topographischen Gegebenheiten eines Ortes auszuloten, zu nutzen und weiterzuentwickeln. Die Ausstellung zeigt aber auch seine zahlreichen Wettbewerbsbeiträge insbesondere für Schulbauten. Ernst Kaspers Lehrtätigkeit wird anschaulich in einer filmischen Dokumentation vermittelt: Ehemalige Schüler kommentieren seine Persönlichkeit und die Art seiner Architekturvermittlung. Die Ausstellung wird durch Kaspers

Ingeborg Flagge
Foreword

On the occasion of Ernst Kasper's 70th birthday, the Aktuelle Galerie in Deutsches Architektur Museum is presenting the first solo show dedicated to his oeuvre. Ernst Kasper was a professor at the Düsseldorf Academy of Art, where he taught for 28 years. Entire generations of architects feared him and revered him, and were strongly influenced by his ideas. To this day, Ernst Kasper continues to run his own architectural office in Aachen. Ernst Kasper and his architecture have always been an inside tip and for many his oeuvre remains to be discovered. The reason: Kasper has been the absolute exception in a world of architects hell-bent on publishing their work. He has tackled his projects quietly, but resolutely – and countless first prizes attest to the fact that juries were fully aware of the outstanding quality of his designs.

The exhibition in the DAM highlights two areas:
It showcases the buildings Kasper created that have been realized, first and foremost among them the Kaiserbad Complex in Aachen, a striking example of his marvelous ability to explore the special topographical details of a site, to exploit them and advance them. The exhibition also displays his countless submissions to competitions, in particular for school buildings. Ernst Kasper's teaching is visualized by a documentary film in which former students comment on his personality and on how he went about

ausdrucksstarke Zeichnungen bestimmt, Zeichnungen, die an Einprägsamkeit und Sensibilität ihresgleichen suchen. Der Besucher erlebt die Ausstellung quasi wie einen Werkstattbesuch, so als sei er zufällig in Kaspers Büro geraten und dürfe in die geöffneten Schubladen hineinschauen.

Das Deutsche Architektur Museum ist glücklich, die Arbeiten Ernst Kaspers, bisher 73 Projekte mit 17 Modellen aus den Jahren 1966 bis 2005, nach dem Ende der Ausstellung in sein Archiv aufnehmen zu dürfen. Es kann mit diesem wichtigen Vertreter der Architektur des ausgehenden 20. Jahrhunderts im Rheinland jenseits der Postmoderne, die das DAM Archiv bisher maßgeblich prägt, eine Lücke in seiner Sammlung schließen.

familiarizing them with architecture. The exhibition also features Kasper's highly expressive drawings, drawings that are quite unprecedented in terms of sensitivity and poignancy. The exhibition thus functions as a kind of workshop into which the visitor enters as if he or she had by chance stepped into Kasper's office and had been permitted to leaf through the open drawers.

Deutsches Architektur Museum is very happy that after the end of the exhibition the works by Ernst Kasper (to date 73 projects and 17 models dating from 1966-2005) will become part of the museum archives. With this important representative of Rhineland architecture from the second half of the last century that eschews all the frills of the postmodern, a movement that has otherwise strongly shaped the face of the DAM, we are closing a gap in our collection.

Susanne Gross
Der Architekt und Architekturlehrer

Die Ausstellung und das begleitende Buch sollen das Werk und die Person des Architekten und Architekturlehrers Ernst Kasper aufspüren. Es ist kein abgeschlossenes Werk, denn Kasper ist als Architekt weiterhin tätig. Insofern ist dies auch kein abschließender Kommentar zu seiner Lehrtätigkeit. Denn er setzt diese nach 28 Jahren an der Klasse Baukunst der Kunstakademie Düsseldorf und nach seiner Emeritierung an anderem Ort fort, an der Scuola Arquitectura in Valdivia, Chile.

Warum soll die Ausstellung „aufspüren"? Weil E. K. über das Rheinland hinaus noch wenig bekannt ist, zu wenig für seine Bauten und Entwürfe und die Generationen von Architekturstudenten, die er geprägt hat.

Ernst Kasper hat über seine Arbeiten nie viele Worte gemacht. So existiert kaum ein veröffentlichter Text von ihm und nur wenige Dokumentationen über seine Arbeiten. Es kursieren allerdings verschiedene, unter seinen ehemaligen Studenten eifersüchtig bewachte Lose-Blatt-Sammlungen von Skizzen, Modellaufnahmen, Wettbewerbszeichnungen. Diese „Raubkopien" für einen eingeweihten Kreis können nun durch die Ausstellung und den Katalog erweitert und öffentlich zugänglich gemacht werden.

Die Person und das Werk Ernst Kaspers nehmen eine Sonderstellung ein, wo auch immer man sie in einen Zusammenhang stellen will. Als Lehrer an der Kunstakademie lehrte Kasper gleichzeitig mit Stirling, Hollein, Ungers, Ortner, Zenghelis, um nur einige zu nennen. Im Lauf der Jahrzehnte gewann er die nie ausgesprochene Stellung einer grauen Eminenz. Er lebte aus der Akademie und er litt, wenn er, was gelegentlich der Fall war, ihren Niedergang befürchten musste. Er war eine Integrationsfigur, und nach seinem Weggang entstand eine Lücke.

Als Lehrer war er unkalkulierbar. Man wusste nie, auf welchen wunden Punkt sein knapper Kommentar zu einer Arbeit zielen würde. Dennoch war es ein Anreiz dafür, sich immer wieder in seine Gefahrenzone zu begeben, die man meinte, bei anderen Lehrern präziser eingrenzen zu können.

Susanne Gross
The Architect and Teacher of Architecture

The exhibition and accompanying catalogue endeavor to throw light on Ernst Kasper the architect, architecture professor, and his oeuvre. For the sake of accuracy we should say his oeuvre to date as Kasper continues to work as an architect. As such this text cannot be a final comment on his career as a professor. After 28 years teaching architecture at the Düsseldorf Academy of Art and his distinction as emeritus professor, Ernst continues his lecturing work at the Scuola Arquitectura in Valdivia, Chile.

Why should the exhibition seek to spotlight this man? Quite simply because he is little known beyond the Rhineland, too little when you consider his buildings, designs and the generations of architecture students he has influenced.

Ernst Kasper never wasted many words on his designs. Which explains the dearth of publications by the architect and the relatively little documentation on his oeuvre. However, there are various collections of loose sheets in circulation jealously guarded by his former students, and which include sketches, photos of models and competition drawings. Now these "pirate copies" only familiar to a privileged few are being presented along with other works in an exhibition and catalogue, making them available to a wider public.

No matter in which context you place them, the person and work of Ernst Kaspers occupy a special position. During his time at the Academy of Art, Kasper taught alongside the likes of Stirling, Hollein, Ungers, Ortner, Zenghelis, to name just a few. Down through the decades, he came to be considered as one of the grand old men of the Academy. His life revolved around the Academy world, and he suffered on those occasions when its demise was to be feared. He tended to be a teacher who brought people together, and his departure left a real vacuum to be filled.

As a teacher he was unpredictable. You never knew which sore spot he would hit with his brief comment on a work. Yet such

Er vertrat keine bestimmte Schule, hatte weder einen vorrangig theoretischen noch einen bestimmten formalen Ansatz. Sein eigenes entwerferisches Denken war bar jeden schematischen Ansatzes. Die einzige verbindliche Kategorie für ihn war der Ort, in den ein Entwurf eingearbeitet werden sollte.

Dass der Ort durch den entwerferischen Eingriff notwendigerweise verändert würde, nahm er in Kauf. Er suchte jedoch, auch in den Arbeiten seiner Studenten, nicht die Veränderung als Selbstzweck, sondern die substantielle Veränderung. Dies war für ihn keine Frage des Bauvolumens. Ein noch so kleiner Eingriff in den Ort konnte diesen Anspruch schon einlösen, eine einzelne Tür, eine Wand, ein kleiner topographischer Versatz.

Die Bedeutung des Ortes – ein fast schon moralischer Anspruch – konnte aber für ihn auch darin münden, dass man ihn, den Ort, ganz anders weiterformte, als man ihn vorgefunden hatte. Dann konnte alles aus den Fugen geraten, um zu einer neuen Ordnung zu finden.

Als Architekt ergibt sich Ernst Kaspers Sonderstellung aus einer schon früh von allen Trends abgelösten baukünstlerischen Entwicklung.

Seine ersten bekannten Entwürfe stammen aus den siebziger Jahren. In den realisierten Berufsschulen in Kempen und Viersen 1975 – 1977 scheinen bekannte Anordnungsmuster dieser Architekturperiode durch: repetitive Muster, meist auf orthogonalen Strukturen basierend. Deutlich gliedernd, bilden sie in erster Linie ihre innere Organisation ab. Achsenverdrehungen von einzelnen Systemabschnitten erzeugen Eingangssituationen und setzen die Bauwerke unter Spannung, so etwa beim Gymnasium in Mönchengladbach 1978 und dem Museumsentwurf in Aachen 1979.

Die Bauten aus dieser Werkphase haben sorgfältig abgestimmte Proportionen, der Goldene Schnitt lässt die Fassaden fast klassisch wirken. In die Reihe lassen sich auch die Justizbehörde in Dortmund

appraisals were a constant incentive to venture into the danger zone, the exact nature of which seemed easier to discern in other professors.

Kasper has never championed a specific school, or pursued a favored theoretical or specific formal approach. His creative thinking is devoid of any systematic pattern. The only binding aspect for him is the location into which a design is to be embedded.

Though he accepts as logical that the location will be altered through his intervention as an architect he does not pursue change for change's sake – either in his own work or that of his students. The change he seeks is substantial, but is not expressed in the extent of the intervention. Even a small intervention in a place might have the desired effect, a single door, a wall, a minor topographical shift.

Yet the importance of the place – which assumes almost moral dimensions for him – might equally result in it being elaborated into something completely different. Then everything gets turned upside down in order to achieve a fresh order.

Ernst Kasper's special status as an architect results from his highly individual development from an early stage onwards; he has remained independent of other architectural trends.

His first well-known plans date back to the 1970s. The vocational colleges realized in Kempen and Viersen 1975-7 reveal some of the compositional styles typical for this architectural period: repetitive patterns generally based on orthogonal structures. The latter have a distinct structural effect and reflect their internal organization. Twisting the axes of individual sections creates new entrance settings and lends the buildings an exciting vibrancy, as in the grammar school in Mönchengladbach 1978 or the museum in Aachen 1979.

1980, das Rathaus in Viersen 1978, das Polizeigebäude in Viersen 1990 einordnen. Alle diese Entwürfe wurden mit ersten Preisen ausgezeichnet, die meisten wurden realisiert.

Und dann lässt sich bei Ernst Kasper, erst ganz subtil und dann immer vehementer, eine Ablösung aus der Zweidimensionalität entdecken. Während sich die allgemeine architektonische Entwicklung in die Postmoderne und damit auch in die Motivsuche für die bauliche Oberfläche begibt, beschreitet er ganz andere Wege. Er beginnt, in die Geometrien seiner Bauwerke die dritte Dimension als dynamisierendes Element einzuführen.

Er nutzt diese Dimension dazu, die immer als Gefüge aus Einzelelementen erscheinenden Kompositionen räumlich regelrecht aus den Angeln zu heben.

Diese Entwicklung beginnt mit dem Entwurf zur Schnellengasse in Eschweiler. Bei diesem Entwurf lösen sich die üblichen Kategorien von Wand, Dach und Boden gänzlich auf; an ihre Stellen tritt eine freie, fast bildhauerische Auffassung des Raumes. Man mag das Entstehungsjahr 1978 für eine so freie Arbeit kaum glauben. Sie war mehr als ein Entwurf, sie war ein räumliches Ereignis.

Ein kurzes Aufflackern, dann tritt diese Linie in den Hintergrund, um sich in den Entwürfen seit 1990 umso deutlicher herauszuschälen. Stellvertretend genannt für diese Arbeiten von größter bildnerischer Kraft seien die Entwürfe zu Halle Spitze, die Synagoge und dann auch das Kaiserbad in Aachen. Die Hallenser Arbeit wurde leider nie realisiert. Sie war mit ihren in eine bühnenhafte Plattform eingearbeiteten Solitären jedoch Vorreiter für eine gänzlich andere Auffassung von Stadt: Der Boden hebt sich aus sich selbst heraus und wird zum Bauwerk der ersten Ebene, aus der dann die zweite Architekturebene erst erwächst.

Beim Aachener Kaiserbad, das bis 1996 realisiert wurde, kommt Kaspers Haltung zum Ort besonders deutlich zum Ausdruck. Eine Gruppe von schiefwinkligen, prismatischen Baukörpern, scheinbar ohne

The buildings from this phase have carefully coordinated proportions, the golden section makes the façades appear almost classical. We can also include in this category the Law Court in Dortmund 1980, the Town Hall in Viersen 1978 and the police HQ in Viersen 1990. All of these designs were awarded first prizes, and most of them were realized.

But subsequently a very subtle and later increasingly vehement move away from the two dimensional is evident in Ernst Kasper's work. Although architecture in general back then drifted into Postmodernism and the search for suitable subject matter for the surface of buildings, Kasper treads totally new paths; he begins to introduce the third dimension into the geometries of his buildings in order to lend them a dynamic element.

By adding this dimension he effectively removes his compositions – which always resemble a structure of individual elements – from their moorings.

His first use of this device occurs in his plan for the Schnellengasse in Eschweiler in which he completely abandons the standard categories of wall, roof and floor; they are replaced by a liberal, almost sculptural approach to space. It is difficult to believe that such an individual work could be created back in 1978. It was not merely a design but a spatial experience.

Following its brief, dramatic appearance this style fades into the background once more, in order to emerge all the more clearly in his designs from 1990 onwards. In this context, we can see the expression of his highly imaginative powers in his designs for Spitze, Halle, the synagogue but also the Kaiserbad in Aachen. Unfortunately the project for Halle was never realized, because it pioneered a totally new concept of a city with its single buildings integrated into a stage-like platform: the ground rises up out of itself to become the edifice of the first level from which the second level then develops.

Regelhaftigkeit, formt ihre eigene Mitte. Und dennoch dient sie als Gesamtkomposition einer übergeordneten Idee: Alles an diesem Gefüge bereitet den großartigen Blick über sich selbst hinweg auf den Aachener Dom vor. Damit wird das Grundstück dynamisch in den Raum verlängert, denn sein unmittelbarer Bezugspunkt liegt weit außerhalb.

Es war für uns Akademieschüler ein Erlebnis, dabei zu sein, wie der virtuose Zeichner Ernst Kasper seinen Stift auf einem Blatt vor sich her trieb und dabei die Räume gedanklich entstehen ließ. Zu lehren und zu bauen ist für ihn eins. Aus dieser Integrität entsteht die große Ausstrahlung seiner Person und seines Werkes.

The Kaiserbad in Aachen, completed in 1996, vividly illustrates Kasper's attitude to location. A group of oblique-angled, prismatic structures seemingly lacking in regularity forms the center and focal point. Simultaneously, it serves as the general composition of an overarching idea: everything in this composition prepares you for the magnificent view out over it towards Aachen Cathedral. As a result, the plot is extended and elongated given that its point of reference lies at considerable distance beyond it.

For us Academy students it was always a special experience to be present when the brilliant draftsman Ernst Kasper let his pen run over a piece of paper and gave shape to his ideas. Teaching and designing are inseparable for him. And it is this sense of unity which accounts for his charismatic personality and the fascination of his work.

Alfonso Hüppi
Ein Aquarell für Ernst Kasper

Nicht dass er schon mit einem architektonischen Raster zur Welt gekommen wäre, vielmehr kommt die Welt zu ihm und er geht mit ihr um wie ein Kind: spielend. Rührt daher die Leichtigkeit seiner Bauten, daher die Freude, mit der man sie betrachtet und sich in ihnen bewegt? Wie schafft er es, dass in seinem Werk kein Zufall herrscht?

Ernst Kasper besucht mich im Atelier, zeigt auf ein Aquarell, das da schon seit zwanzig Jahren unbeachtet zwischen all dem Aufgehäuften liegt. „Die Farben – die Maße", so sein Kommentar. „Ich schenke es dir."

Aber die Maße? Dass er, selber ein Meister der Farbe, auf diese hinweist, kann ich verstehen. Doch die Maße? Keinen Gedanken habe ich während des Malens darauf verwendet. Er nimmt einen herumliegenden Zettel, setzt ihn an, legt die Diagonale, die Senkrechte, die Waagerechte: „Alles hängt mit allem zusammen", belehrt er mich. Ganz im Nebenbei öffnet er mir vor dem unscheinbaren Objekt die Augen für mein selbstvergessenes Tun.

Das ist Ernst Kasper, Maß nehmend und Maß gebend, doch offen für das Zufallende, knapp in der Sprache, präzise in der Analyse. Wann immer man mit ihm ins Gespräch kommt, alles endet oder beginnt mit dem Maß, führt zu den Zusammenhängen, und wir ahnen, was für ein großartiger Lehrer er sein muss.

Alfonso Hüppi
A water-color for Ernst Kasper

It is not that he entered this world with an architect's eye, but rather that the world comes to him, and his treatment of it is playful, childlike. Does this account for the lightness of his buildings, our delight in looking at them and moving in them? How does he manage to keep chance out of his works?

Ernst Kasper visits me in my studio, points to a water-color that has languished unnoticed for twenty years amongst the piles. "The colors – the proportions," he remarks. "It's yours".

But the proportions? It's understandable this master of colors should refer to them but the proportions? I gave them no thought at all while I was painting. He picks up a piece of paper, uses it to trace the diagonal, the vertical, the horizontal: "Everything is connected with everything else," he explains to me. Standing in front of this nondescript object executed while lost in thought he proceeds with great casualness to open up my eyes for it.

That is Ernst Kasper, taking measure and setting standards, yet open to the accidental, terse in his language, precise in his analysis. Whenever you get into conversation with him everything revolves around measurements, leads to the connections, and we realize what a brilliant teacher he must be.

Unterwegs in Italien, das Hebammenköfferchen mit dem Malzeug zu Füßen, hält er die Silhouette einer Landschaft fest, setzt die Umrisse und Kuben, Unsicherheiten gibt es nicht. Sein Auge ist geschult, er sieht, was ist und seine Phantasie baut weiter an dem, was sein wird. Mitten in der Toskana, umgeben vom Wohlklang italienischer Sprache, tönt es in markantestem Deutsch: „Scheiße!" Ernst Kasper steht vor dem geöffneten Kofferraum seines Wagens. Darin schwimmen seine Klamotten im kaltgepressten Olivenöl. Extra vergine. Er sieht das Desaster und bricht in Lachen aus. Die Maßlosigkeit der Bescherung versetzt ihn in heitere Betrachtung. Er blickt nicht in den Abgrund einer Aporie, er sieht im Chaos die Möglichkeit. Da haben wir's, „alles hängt mit allem zusammen". In diesem Fall ist ein maroder Korken die Ursache zur Gleichung der Differenz.

Ernst Kasper siebzig? – endlich – so gewinnt unser Lachen einen würdigen Nachhall ...

On the road in Italy, the midwife's bag containing his painting utensils at his feet he captures the silhouette of a landscape, deftly defines the outlines and volumes, there is no uncertainty. His eye is well trained, he sees what is there and his imagination adds the details that will complete the picture. In the heart of Tuscany, alive with the sound of melodious Italian, a voice rings out in harsh, cutting German: "Damn!". Ernst Kasper stands in front of the open boot of his car. Inside his clothes float amid cold-pressed olive oil. Extra virgin. He eyes the disaster and bursts out laughing. The excessive nature of the mess strikes him as funny. He does not stare into the depths of an irresolvable paradox but sees the opportunities in chaos. There we have it, "Everything is connected with everything". In this case a faulty cork sufficed to eradicate the difference.

Ernst Kasper seventy? – About time. Now our laughter is lent a dignified echo.

Laurids Ortner
Pulcinella

Es muss in den achtziger Jahren des vergangenen Jahrhunderts
gewesen sein, als der Wechsel vom Pinocchio ins Pulcinella erfolgte. In
der Regel am Dienstag traf man sich dort zum Mittagessen. Damals war
noch Hans Hollein dabei. Zu viel Knoblauch, sagt Ernst Kasper, war der
Grund für den Wechsel. Er und Erwin Heerich entschieden sich fürs
Pulcinella. Auf der Ratinger Straße, um etwa dreißig Schritte näher in
Richtung Düsseldorfer Kunstakademie. Dass man zu Fuß auf kurzem
Weg von der Akademie zum Mittagessen gehen konnte, war erste
Wichtigkeit, dass es ein Italiener ist zweite, Qualität des Essens dritte,
des Weines vierte, der gute Kellner fünfte, als letzte das Lokal selbst, so
wie es aussah – seine Architektur. Auch darin unterschieden sich die
beiden nicht wesentlich: auf rustikal gemacht, eng unterteilt, dunkel-
braune Holztische und Bänke. Der Gipsputz im Pinocchio bildete ein
wogendes Meer von ca. fünf Zentimeter langen Spitzen, im Pulcinella
war es eine in Tellergröße geschüsselte Oberfläche. Wahrscheinlich war
diese weiblichere Wandformation ausschlaggebend, dass sich nun hier
seit gut zwanzig Jahren die Architekturprofessoren der Kunstakademie
mehr oder minder wöchentlich zum Mittagessen treffen.

Das Pulcinella hat sich in all den Jahren nicht verändert. Von der hellen
Straße tritt man in einen schmalen, langgestreckten Raum. Die dunkel-
braunen Bänke und Tische stehen coupéförmig senkrecht zu den
beiden Längswänden. Das Tageslicht, das durch die straßenseitigen
Fensterscheiben kommt, reicht gerade für die drei Tische am Fenster.
Zwischen den Tischen ein knapper Gang, man geht auf eine kleine
schwarze Bar zu, deren Stellage mit Flaschen und Gläsern an die dunkle
Holzdecke reicht. Dahinter, in einer kleinen Nische mit Fenster zur
Straße, hantiert der Pizzakoch vor seinem Ofen. Linkerhand geht es
durch eine mit Gipskarton verkleidete Holzkonstruktion, in dem auch die
Mäntel aufgehängt werden, in den nächsten Essraum. Wellenförmig
gebogene Kupferrohre mit Glühbirnen an den Enden geben schumm-
riges Licht, an das sich das Auge trotz des gedämpften Vorraumes erst
anpassen muss. Und da steht die Akademietafel: vier der Länge nach
zusammengestellte Bistrotische mit einer zusätzlichen Einhängeplatte. An

Laurids Ortner
Pulcinella

The changeover from Pinocchio to Pulcinella must have happened
in the 1980s. They generally met there on Tuesdays for lunch. And
back then the party included Hans Hollein. According to Ernst
Kasper the reason for the change was too much garlic. He and
Erwin Heerich decided on Pulcinella. It was in Ratinger Strasse,
some 30 meters closer to the Düsseldorf Academy of Art. The first
point in its favor was that lunching there only involved a short walk
from the Academy, secondly it was Italian, third came the quality of
the food, fourth the wine, fifth the good waiter, and finally the
restaurant itself, its appearance – its architecture. In this final point
the two also differed little: a rustic look, divided into small sections,
dark brown wooden tables and benches. The stucco work in
Pinocchio formed an undulating sea of roughly 5 cm long peaks, in
Pulcinella it was a surface made up of plate-sized swirls.
Presumably this more feminine wall decoration was the major
reason why architecture professors from the Art Academy met here
once a week for lunch for a good 20 years.

In all those years Pulcinella did not change. Coming in from the
bright street you enter a narrow, elongated room. The dark brown
benches and tables stand in a sloping line with the two long walls.
The daylight that enters through the windows facing the street is
just sufficient for the three tables at the window. There is a narrow
passage between the tables, you approach a small, black bar
whose racks with bottles and glasses extend as far as the dark
wooden ceiling. At the back in a small niche with a window onto the
street the pizza baker bustles about in front of his oven. To the left
you pass through a wooden structure clad with plaster board that is
also used for hanging up coats, into the next dining room. Wavy,
curved copper tubes sporting light-bulbs give off a dim light that
takes some adjusting to despite the subdued light in the first room.
It is here that the Academy table stands: four bistro tables standing
end to end lengthwise plus a connecting table top. Against the long
wall whose right section contains an inset glass shelf as a window

der Längswand, in deren rechtem Teil ein Glasregal als Fenster zur Bar eingeschnitten ist, eine schmale lange Bank. Bis zu acht Personen lassen sich hier auffädeln, heraus kommt allerdings keiner, bevor die Tafel aufgehoben ist. Die Wandbank endet an ihrem linken Ende hakenförmig und bildet in einer holzverkleideten Nische, die kaum breiter als der Tisch ist, den Kopf der Tafel. Hier saß Kasper die meiste Zeit. „Jetzt sitzt der Lüpertz immer auf meinem Patz."

Über all die Jahre wechselten einige Besitzer. Gut gelaunte Kellner, denen man Brocken Italienisch zuwarf, waren wieder weg, wenn man begann, sie ins Herz zu schließen. Die Küche schwankte geringfügig, was die Qualität betraf. Aber es konnte passieren, dass von einem Tag auf den anderen die Speisekarte umgekrempelt war. Die wenigen Gerichte, auf die man sich eingestellt hatte, gab es nicht mehr. Das war dann der neue Besitzer. An der Einrichtung aber änderte sich nichts. Einmal wurden kleinere farbige Zeichnungen aufgehängt, die der Besitzer selbst gemacht hatte oder ein Freund von ihm.

Natürlich gab es immer wieder Anläufe, das Lokal zu wechseln. James Stirling waren die Bänke zu schmal und unbequem, O. M. Ungers war generell eher selten zum Mittagessen zu bewegen („Meine Frau hat mir zu wenig Geld mitgegeben"), Josef Paul Kleihues konnte sich nie so recht mit dem Ambiente abfinden. Und Elia Zenghelis waren zu Beginn diese Mittagessen überhaupt suspekt. Gewohnt an den angelsächsischen Drill der Architectural Association in London, schien ihm diese Mittagsakademie eine merkwürdige Form von Zeitvergeudung. Man ging gegen eins zum Essen und kehrte gegen vier Uhr auf die Akademie zurück. Zeit genug, um untereinander und mit dazugeladenen Studenten alles außer Architektur zu besprechen. Architektur tauchte als direktes Thema nur selten auf. Am ehesten, wenn der Kunsthistoriker Walter Hofmann eingriff und detaillierte geschichtliche Bezüge darlegte. Sonst aber ergab sich das Gespräch wie an anderen Wirtshaustischen aus dem Tagesgeschehen.

to the bar, stands a long, narrow bench. Up to eight people can squeeze in here, but nobody can leave until the table has been cleared. The left section of the bench ends in a hook: occupying a wood-paneled niche scarcely broader than the table, it forms the head of the table. This was where Kasper generally sat. "Now Lüpertz always sits in my place."

In all the years it changed hands several times. Amiable waiters to whom you tossed a few scraps of Italian left as soon as you had begun to grow fond of them. The cuisine varied only slightly as regards quality, but it could happen that from one day to the next the menu was changed completely. And then the few meals you had got used to were no longer served. A new owner had taken charge. But the furnishings remained unchanged. Once smallish, colored drawings created by the owner or a friend of his appeared on the walls.

Naturally, there were repeated attempts to go somewhere else. James Stirling found the benches too narrow and uncomfortable, O. M. Ungers could seldom be persuaded to join us for lunch ("My wife hasn't given me enough money"), Josef Paul Kleihues never really liked the atmosphere. And initially Elia Zenghelis was sceptical about the whole idea of these lunches. Accustomed to the Anglo-Saxon drill of the Architectural Association in London, he considered these Academy lunches to be a remarkable waste of time. They set off just before one o'clock and returned to the Academy just before four. Time enough to chat among themselves and with the invited students about everything but architecture. Only seldom did architecture crop up as a specific topic. Mostly when art historian Walter Hofmann butted in and elaborated detailed historical references. But otherwise as in other pubs the day's events provided the subjects of conversation.

Ernst Kasper vertraute diesem Prinzip der Annäherung instinktiv: über die Auseinandersetzung mit dem Alltäglichen zu einer verfeinerten Besonderheit zu gelangen. Wenn er im Zusammenhang mit dem Schaffen von Architektur wiederholt von der dafür „notwendigen Sinnlichkeit" sprach, so bezog sich das zuallererst auf eine anteilnehmende Wahrnehmung des Alltäglichen, aus der sich erst alle Verfeinerungen zum Besonderen ergeben können.

Kasper mochte keine Richtungen und doktrinären Ansätze. Auch Ordnung als kollektives Prinzip schien ihm verdächtig. Für seine Bauten nutzte er erprobte geometrische Proportionssysteme, größere übergreifende Regelungen standen aber immer im Verdacht, fatale alte Denkmuster zurückzuholen. Brachte man doch ab und zu das Thema auf Gemeinsamkeiten und Qualitäten einer neuen deutschen Architektur – die doch haushoch unterschätzt sei in Europa und der Welt –, da war bei aller gegenseitigen Wertschätzung eine Schattenlinie erreicht. Kasper ist überzeugt von der genialen Möglichkeit des Individuums. Die Wege dorthin sind nur mit Strenge, mit Sorgfalt und Hartnäckigkeit zu erreichen, und doch muss zuletzt eine spielerisch leichte, großzügige Konzeption herauskommen. Aber solch fundamentalistisches Geplänkel gab es nur sporadisch. Der Stil des Miteinandersprechens war feiner. So ruppig mancher Satz sich anhörte, so dröhnend das Lachen folgte, so behutsam war doch alles darauf abgestimmt, niemanden zu belehren und doch dabei die eigene Vielfalt zu äußern. Zum Vorschein kamen dann Personen, die im Nu aus dem alltäglich Banalen eigenwillige scharfe Überlegungen in freiere Dimensionen herstellten. Gespräche dieser Art versuchten nichts zu erklären. Sie waren eher der Anlass, den anderen einen kurzen Blick in die eigene Komplexität zu gewähren.

Ernst Kasper instinctively trusted this approach of starting with the everyday and the general in order to arrive at something more sophisticated and specific. If when speaking about the creation of architecture he repeatedly spoke of the "necessary appeal to the senses" he was referring first and foremost to an interested, sympathetic perception of the everyday, which must exist if you are to move from it to the specific.

Kasper thought nothing of styles or doctrinaire approaches. He was also somewhat dubious about order as a collective principle. For his buildings he used tried and tested geometrical proportion systems; but there was always a danger that more general rules would mean the return of fatal, old patterns of thinking. All the same, the talk sometimes turned to their common interest in and the qualities of a new, German architecture – which was nonetheless hugely underrated in Europe and the world – for all the mutual appreciation, opinion is divided. Kasper is convinced of the individual's potential genius. This potential is only achieved through discipline, precision and persistence; yet ultimately the final result must be a playfully light, generous conception.
However, such fundamental skirmishes only occurred sporadically. The style of debate and interaction was subtler. No matter how coarse some sentences sounded, or how loud the subsequent laughter was, everything was carefully orchestrated to allow the expression of individual diversity without anyone feeling lectured. As a result lunch participants could move swiftly from the banal and everyday to produce highly individual, keen reflections in a wider context. Talks of this nature made no attempt at explanation; instead, they were a vehicle for granting the others a brief insight into your own complexity.

Im Lauf der Zeit mauserten sich diese Mittagessen zu einer Art akademischer Institution, ohne dass irgend jemand darauf besonderen Wert gelegt hätte. An manchen Tagen lud Rektor Markus Lüpertz zum Mittagessen und das Pulcinella war voll mit den Künstlern der Akademie. Ausstellungsmacher hätten auf einem Fleck beisammengehabt, wofür sie für ihre Documenta- oder Biennale-Beteiligungen mühselig hätten hinter-herreisen müssen. Versuche, dieses Prinzip direkt in die Akademie zu verpflanzen und das mittägliche Essen am Dienstag für die Architektur-studenten mit Tischgesprächen aufzupäppeln, scheiterten nach einigen Essen. Die Vorbereitungen waren zu aufwändig, letztlich fehlte die Selbstverständlichkeit des Pulcinella. Immerhin hat sich Jahre später daraus die Vortragsreihe der „Tischgespräche" ergeben: Gespräche mit Gästen am Zeichentisch in der Akademie, und nachher zum Italiener.

P u l c i n e l l a könnte ein Passwort sein für den Zugang zu Kaspers Architektur. Ansonsten ist es einfach der nächste Italiener, der zu Fuß von der Akademie erreichbar ist.

In the course of time these lunches turn into something of an academic institution though nobody set out with that intention. On some days Director Markus Lüpertz invited people to lunch and Pulcinella was full of Academy artists. This united on one spot what exhibition makers would normally have to work hard for and chase after to secure contributions to the Documenta or Biennial. Endeavors to transplant this principle onto the Academy itself and to beef up the Tuesday lunches for the architecture students with table talks, failed after a few attempts. The preparations were too time consuming, and the familiar setting, Pulcinella, was missing. For all that, years later the lunches did produce a series of lectures called the 'Table Talks': talks with guests at the drawing board in the Academy followed by a visit to the Italian restaurant.

P u l c i n e l l a could be a password providing access to Kasper's architecture. Or simply the nearest Italian restaurant to be reached on foot from the Academy.

Paul Good
Rhythmus und Detail
im Denken des Architekten Ernst Kasper

Die Architektur und die Philosophie wohnen in der Kunstakademie Düsseldorf auf einer Etage. Das ist in der Sache richtig, weil beide alle Künste einbeziehen. Es kann darüber hinaus auch eine Nähe in der Architektonik des Denkens bei beiden geben. Es traf sich gut, dass der Architekt Ernst Kasper die Liebe zum Detail, die Gebärde der kleinen Dinge wie diejenige einer Tür, einer Treppe, den Verlauf einer Linie, die Wirkung einer Form an einer bestimmten Stelle, die menschlichen Dimensionen und Maße usw., der großen architektonischen Geste vorgezogen hat. Das kam meiner Philosophie entgegen, welche sich der Architektonik der Metaphysik und auch noch derjenigen Kants enthält zu Gunsten eines Denkens der kurzen Formen: des Spruches eines Heraklit, des Paradoxes eines Meister Eckhart, des Aphorismus von Nietzsche, der Bemerkung von Wittgenstein.

Bauwerke sehen lernen: Das war ein Hauptanliegen der Arbeit von Ernst Kasper mit den jungen Menschen. Wo sind die Gewichte, wo entstehen Ungleichgewichte, welches ist der Rhythmus der Formen, wo gibt es Unfertiges, Ungelöstes, Unstimmiges? Egal bei welcher Stilart, bei alten wie bei neuen Bauten. Bauästhetik als Rhythmus und Stimmigkeit im Detail. Konzept und Praxis mussten stimmen. Dazu zählt auch die Umgebung, der Genius loci der bebauten Nachbarschaft, des lebensweltlichen Gebrauchswertes eines Platzes, auch noch die Landschaft und das entfernte Gebirge. Rhythmus im Ganzen, Präzision im Detail.

Paul Good
Rhythm and Detail
in the way of thinking of architect Ernst Kasper

Architecture and Philosophy occupy the same floor at the Academy of Art in Düsseldorf. That is as it should be factually speaking, as both cover all the arts. And there can also be proximity in terms of the architectonics of thought. It was a fortunate coincidence that architect Ernst Kasper preferred the love of detail, the gesture of small things such as those of a door, a staircase, the run of a line, the influence a shape has at a particular point, the human dimensions and measurements to all grand architectural gesture. That was in keeping with my philosophy, which rejects the architectonics of metaphysics or even that of Kant in favor of thinking in abbreviated forms: the sayings of a Heraclitus, the paradoxes of Master Eckhart, the aphorisms of Nietzsche, the remarks of Wittgenstein.

Learning to see buildings – that was a main intention behind what Ernst Kasper sought to convey to young people. Where are the harmonies, where do imbalances arise, what is the rhythm of the shapes, where is something unfinished, unresolved, illogical? Irrespective of the building style, be it old or new edifices. Building aesthetics as rhythm and consistency in the details. Concept and practice must be in line. This includes the surroundings, the genius loci of the architecture of the neighborhood, the utility a location has in the lifeworld, not to forget the landscape and remote mountains. Rhythms for the whole, precision for the details.

Rhythmus ist Atem: Ein Gebäude atmet. Fülle und Leere, Flächen und Volumen, Geraden und Krümmungen, Lastendes und Schwebendes, Verschlossenes und Offenes müssen zusammengehen. Klarheit der Verhältnisse ist ein Hauptwort von Ernst Kasper. Es geht nicht um Stil, es geht um Klarheit.

Der Architekt Kasper konnte die Stadt so schätzen, wie der Philosoph Wittengenstein sie als Bild für die Sprache benutzt hat: „Ein Gewinkel von Gässchen und Plätzen, alten und neuen Häusern, und Häuser mit Zubauten aus verschiedenen Zeiten; und dies umgeben von einer Menge neuer Vororte mit geraden und regelmäßigen Straßen und mit einförmigen Häusern." (Philosophische Untersuchungen Nr. 18) Was bei Wittgenstein für die Sprache und die Bedeutung der Wörter aufgrund des zeitlichen Gebrauchs galt, das betonte Kasper für die Baukunst: eine Architektur vorstellen heißt, sich eine Lebensform vorstellen.

Wir haben zusammen einige auswärtige Seminare mit Kunstexkursionen gemacht. Zwei waren mit der Idee der Falte beschäftigt. Wenn man mit Leibniz davon ausgeht, dass die körperliche Welt nicht wie bei Descartes durch räumliche „Ausdehnung", sondern dadurch definiert ist, dass und wie Kräfte auf Kräfte wirken, dann bekommt man bei der Darstellung dieser Wirkungen, kleiner als die kleinste wahrnehmbare Größe genommen, niemals eine Gerade, sondern stets eine Krümmung, eine Falte. Die Krümmung hält das Konkave und das Konvexe, Innen und

Rhythm is breath: a building breathes. Fullness and emptiness, surfaces and volumes, straight lines and bending curves, borne loads and floating qualities, closure and openness – they must all go together. The clarity of relationships, that is one of Ernst Kasper's main endeavors. The focus is not on style, but on clarity.

Kasper the architect appreciated the city the way philosopher Wittengenstein used it as an image for language: "A maze of little streets and squares, of old and new houses, and of houses with additions from various periods; and this surrounded by a multitude of new boroughs with straight regular streets and uniform houses." (Philosophical Investigations, no. 18) What applied in Wittgenstein's eyes to language and the meaning of words owing to their temporal usage, is what Kasper emphasized for the art of building: imagining an architecture means imagining a form of life.

Together, we ran a few seminars with art excursions away from the Academy. Two concerned themselves with the idea of the fold. If, following Leibniz, we assume that the physical world is not defined, as Descartes would have it, by spatial "extension", but by the fact that forces impact on forces and how this happens, then, when representing these influences, at a level smaller than even the smallest perceptible variable, you never get a straight line, but always a bend, a fold. The bend always unites concave and convex,

Außen, Geist und Materie, stets zusammen, ein räumlich statisches Weltbild löst sich durch ein zeitlich dynamisches ab. Wie falten sich die Kräfte in einem Bau? Das war uns bis in die kleinsten Kleinigkeiten hinein stets ein Hauptanliegen.

Unvergesslich schön steht auch das Seminar zu Paul Valérys „Eupalinos oder der Architekt" hoch oben in Soglio, der Sonnenterrasse im Bergell, in meiner Erinnerung da. Wir waren eine ganze Woche lang in Nebel und Regen eingeschlossen. Der berühmte Bergkranz der Sciora- und Bondascagruppe zeigte sich kein einziges Mal. Valéry hat sein Gespräch zwischen Phaidros und Sokrates im Hades angesiedelt. Da hatten wir unseren Hades im Gebirge! „Was gibt es Geheimnisvolleres als die Klarheit?" Die rhetorische Frage des Dichters war uns augenscheinlich. Aber auch diesen Satz bejahten wir: „Das Schönste, was es gibt, kommt nicht vor in der Ewigkeit." Das Schönste ist nur im Zeitlichen zu haben. Und zu verstehen war, was es heißt, dass unter den Bauwerken einige stumm sind, andere reden, die seltensten sogar singen! Die Säulen-fassaden einiger griechischer Tempel singen sicher. Diese äußerste Belebtheit hängt nicht von der Bestimmung, auch nicht von der allgemeinen Gestalt ab, sondern vom Talent des Erbauers und von der Gunst der Musen. Ernst Kasper ist mit beidem gesegnet. Und die dreihundertjährigen, steinbedeckten Häuser in engen Gässchen von Soglio sangen ihr monotones Lied einer schon musealen Zeit.

inside and outside, mind and matter. A spatially static image of the world gives way to one that is dynamic in time. How do forces fold in a building was always one of our main interests down the very smallest details.

In my memory, how unforgettably beautiful the seminar on Paul Valéry's "Eupalinos or the Architect", high up in Soglio, that sunny veranda in Bergell. We were enclosed by mist and rain for an entire week. The famous crown of the Sciora and Bondasca mountains did not appear once. Valéry placed his debate between Phaidros and Socrates in Hades. And we had our Hades in the mountains! "What more mysterious a thing is there than clarity?" The poet's rhetorical question lay before our eyes. Yet we also affirmed the following statement: "The most beautiful thing there is does not exist in eternity." The beautiful exists only in time. And another thing to be grasped was what it meant to say that some buildings are dumb, others talk, and the rare few sing! The columned façades of some Greek temples most certainly sing. This extreme vibrancy does not hinge on their purpose, nor on their general shape, but on the talent of the builder and the favor of the Muses. Ernst Kasper is blessed with both. And the 300-year-old, stone covered houses in the narrow alleys of Soglio sang their monotonous song of a time that was already confined to museums.

Die Studienfahrt mit Düsseldorfer und mit Maastrichter Architektur-studierenden nach Volterra, der Etruskerstadt, geriet, was das Ergebnis auf dem Papier betraf, aufgrund der großen Zahl vielleicht etwas aus dem Ruder, war aber ein grandioser Erfolg in der Kunst des Zusammen-sehens von Bau- und Lebensform. Die Fassade des „Palazzo dei Priori" lässt an Klarheit nichts zu wünschen übrig, obwohl der Rhythmus von Flächen und Öffnungen auf jeder der drei Etagen offensichtlich keinem einheitlichen Ganzen unterliegt. Wie Heterogenität auch eine Harmonie stiften kann, wurde hier zum Erlebnis.

Ein Dankeschön! Ein Glückwunsch zum runden Geburtstag! Noch eine Exkursion mit Philosophie! Und weiterhin den Humor, den wir bei Ernst Kasper stets genossen haben!

The study trips with architecture students from Düsseldorf and Maastricht to "Volterra", that Etruscan city, on occasion got slightly out of hand perhaps as regards the results on paper, owing to the large numbers of participants, but were a marvelous success in the art of seeing forms of buildings and life together. The façade of the "Palazzo dei Priori" leaves nothing to be desired as regards clarity, although the rhythm of surfaces and openings quite manifestly does not form a united whole on each of the three floors. Here, the result was how heterogeneity can also foster harmony.

Many thanks! And congratulations on your 70th! Here's to another excursion with philosophy! And lot's more Ernst Kasper humor, which we have always so enjoyed!

G. H. Holländer
Schweigende Gärten

„Dieses Werk war ein Ärgernis, denn Verwirrung und Wunder sind Taten,
die sich für Gott gehören, nicht für Menschen."
BORGES, Die zwei Könige und die zwei Labyrinthe

Die Arbeiten des Architekten werden als Zeichnung wiederhergestellt. In
der Wirklichkeit kommen sie außerhalb ihres Zusammenhangs nicht vor,
da sie nicht beweglich sind. Sie sind Teil einer mineralischen Art von
Botanik. Nicht zufällig verfügen Architekten – wenigsten die Baumeister
unter ihnen wie Ernst Kasper – über Instinkte, die in der Kunst des
Paradiesbaus aufgehen. Sie befassen sich mit dem Wachstum der
Steine, sorgen sich um seltene Pflanzen wie ums gemeine Gras; die
besten wissen auch mit dem Unkraut umzugehen, mit der schlechten
Nachbarschaft, die der Mensch nun mal zum Leben braucht. Trotzdem
überrascht mich das Gleichnis, es ist unbeabsichtigt und nun werde ich
es nicht los; aber Kaspers Arbeiten, von denen ich jetzt Photographien
und Zeichnungen sehe, ob ich sie aus der Wirklichkeit kenne oder nicht,
enthalten ein Echo anderer Erfahrungen, die das Gleichnis plausibel
machen, eine selbstgemachte Idee von Architektur, vom Leben der
Steine. So beobachte ich also den Gärtner, groß und zugleich gebeugt,
so wie jeder, der sich den Dingen zuneigt, statt seine Nase hoch zu
tragen, voller Stolz natürlich, wie Gärtner so sind, schweigsam, aber
beredt und unmöglich zu widerlegen.

Das Schweigen ist wichtig. Steine sind still, sie sprechen in geo-
metrischen Sätzen, die oft unvollständig oder elliptisch sind. Der
Architekt zeichnet auf, wie ihre Nachreden, ihr Murmeln, ihr hoher Ton
sich je nachdem fortsetzen ließen, wobei er eine dingliche Form von
Geschichtlichkeit zum Vorschein kommen lässt, ein unbewegtes
Schauspiel der Zeit. Mir gefallen Kaspers Schulgebäude in

G. H. Holländer
The Silent Gardens

"This work was a scandal since confusion and miracles are
operations that belong to God and not to Man.
BORGES, The two kings and the two labyrinths

The architect's works are reconstructed as drawings. In the real
world they do not occur outside their context, being immobile. They
are part of a mineral sort of botanology. It is not by chance that
architects – at least those who are master builders, like Ernst
Kasper – possess instincts that evolve towards the art of Paradise.
They are concerned with the growth of stones, taking care both of
rare plants and plain grass; the best of them know how to cope
with weeds, with the bad neighbourhood that Man inevitably needs
to live in. All the same, the simile takes me by surprise, it is un-
intended, and now I cannot shake it off; but Kasper's works of
which I now see photographs and drawings, whether I know them
from reality or not, contain an echo of other experiences that make
the simile plausible, an original idea of architecture, of mineral life.
So I observe the gardener, tall and also bent, like every man who
inclines towards things instead of raising his head above them, full
of pride of course, the way gardeners are, taciturn and yet
loquacious and impossible to contradict.

Silences are important. The stones are quiet, speaking in geometrical sentences, often incomplete or elliptical. The architect
records how their denunciations, their murmurings, their high
speech could eventually be continued, letting a material kind of
historicality transpire, an immobile drama of time. I like Kasper's
school buildings at Mönchengladbach because of this sort of
readibility; they contain a library which could be the model of a city,

Mönchengladbach, weil sie diese Art von Lesbarkeit besitzen; sie enthalten eine Bibliothek, die das Modell einer Stadt sein könnte, einer sehr modernen Stadt, die von einem Gebäudekomplex umschlossen ist, der in eine zufällige, zu oft zerstörte und ihres Charakters beraubte Stadtstruktur hineingesetzt ist. Benachbart dem städtebaulichen Desaster von Hans Holleins nach innen gewandten Museumsgebäuden umschließt Kaspers Schule einen Vorschlag für die Zukunft der Stadt, der auch nach fast einer Generation noch brauchbar ist. Tatsächlich ist Architektur ein Theater: von Temperamenten, Jahreszeiten, chirurgischen Schnitten; aber in der Langsamkeit der Handlung verstecken sich die Menschen, die sich schnell, dazwischenhin bewegen. Architekten müssen daher langsam sein, wie Gärtner eben. Wie Ernst Kasper.

Der Gärtner ist ein unbequemer Nachbar. Er untersucht Klima und Boden, denkt sich seltsame Pflanzen aus, die dort gedeihen könnten, hat wenig Geduld mit Leuten, die nicht fähig sind, das aus der Vergangenheit ihnen Aufgegebene zu schätzen, und sich vom schlechten Geschmack zu einer falschen Größe verleiten lassen, die ihrer Stadt nicht bekommt. Denn der Architekt, wenn er ein Gärtner ist, muss stets auch ein Städter sein, Stadtbewohner, Bürger. Auch den kleinsten Ort kann er zur Stadt machen, aber er hat keinen Ort, an dem er das Sagen hat. Er kann seine Stadt lieben, so viel er will, aber sie wird seine Muße nicht teilen, sie bleibt auf Seiten von Macht und Wirtschaft, von denen sie eifersüchtig bewacht wird, so wenig sie sich um ihre Gesundheit auch kümmern. Die Stadt wird sich dem Architekten nur hingeben, wenn

a very modern city enclosed in a complex of buildings set in the haphazard structure of a town too often destroyed and deprived of any character. Next to the urbanistic disaster of Hans Hollein's introvert museum buildings, Kasper's school encapsules a possible urban future which almost a generation later still remains a valid proposition. Architecture, in fact, is a theatre: of temperaments, seasons, surgical sections; but the slowness of the action hides the people that are moving quickly in between. Architects therefore have to move slowly, like gardeners. Like Ernst Kasper.

Gardeners make uncomfortable neighbours. They examine climates and soils, imagining strange plants that might grow there, are impatient with people incapable of valuing what the past has given up to them and who are led by bad taste toward a wrong sort of greatness, unbecoming to their city. This is because the architect, if he is a gardener, must always be urbanized, the inhabitant of a city, a citizen. Even the smallest of places he may turn into a city, but he has no place to rule. He may love his city as much as he likes, but it will not share his rest, it stays on the side of power and commerce who guard it jealously, however little they may care for its health. The city will not submit itself to the architect unless this be unseen by others; his hands do not appear firm enough for a serious affair, however hard the city may have been handled by them, since they remain the hands of a gardener; they lack the attraction of a high-handedness that cannot be found in the considered arbitrariness of reason and invention.

keiner dies sieht; seine Hände scheinen ihr nicht fest genug, so hart er sie auch behandelt haben mag, denn sie bleiben die Hände eines Gärtners; ihnen fehlt die Anziehungskraft einer Willkür, die in der abgewogenen Entschiedenheit von Vernunft und Erfindung nicht zu spüren ist.

So ist es kein Wunder, wenn der Architekt meist ferngehalten wird von Projekten, die er in seiner Stadt inspirieren sollte. Anderswohin wird er gerufen, dort aber denkt er an den Garten, der seiner sein sollte; er begegnet schwierigen Beziehungen ohne Festigkeit; er gewinnt Wettbewerbe, aber es kommt nichts Konkretes dabei heraus, verliert andere und darf bauen. Damit wird das Werk des Architekten tatsächlich ein Garten verlorener und beiläufiger Abenteuer, ein Labyrinth, dessen Mitte aber immer ein bestimmter Ort ist, an dem Ideen und Erinnerungen sich verschränken sollten. Nichtsdestoweniger kann er in dieser Mitte, seinem Utopia, dem selbstgebauten Haus nicht leben. Ein solches Haus, das Haus eines Architekten, war Kaspers erstes ausgereiftes Projekt, das er 1963 als Diplomarbeit vorlegte: der Ausbau und Umbau der Burg in Nideggen. Dieses Projekt ist auch eine Anthologie von Einflüssen, die einem erfahrenen Betrachter klar sind. In diesem Sinne kann der Entwurf für Nideggen, wie die frühe Arbeit jedes Künstlers, als späte Arbeit der Meister betrachtet werden, denen Kasper als Student folgte. Aber ich nenne sie nicht. Oder vielmehr, es gibt da einen Namen, in den diese Namen verschmolzen, in den frühen sechziger Jahren, während einer kurzen und sehr fruchtbaren Periode für alle, die in sie hineingerieten. Eine Zeit, als es einen großen Architekturlehrer an der Aachener Hochschule gab, Steinbach, einen Mythos, der im Werk seiner Studenten nachlebt. Wie Kasper.

So it is no wonder that the architect will usually be kept at a distance from projects in the city of which he should be the inspirer. He is called elsewhere, but once there he will remember the garden which should be his; he encounters difficult relationships without stability; he wins competitions which lead to nothing tangible, loses others and is called upon to build. In this way, the architect's work does indeed become a garden of lost and casual adventures, a labyrinth whose center, however, is always a definite place where ideas and recollections should interlock. Nethertheless, in this center, his utopia, the house built by himself, he cannot live. Such a house, an architect's house, was Kasper's first mature project, submitted as a diploma thesis in 1963: the extension and rebuilding of the castle at Nideggen. This project is also an anthology of influences, obvious to any experienced observer. In this sense the Nideggen project, like any artist's early work, may be seen as a later work of the masters that Kasper followed as a student. But I will not name them. Or rather, there is one name into which these names coalesced, in the early sixties, for a short and very productive period for all who got involved. A time when there was a great architectural teacher at Aachen university, Steinbach, a myth who lives on in the work of his students. Like Kasper.

To achieve its own reality, architecture has to express a past which it at the same time replaces, though also a future which it renders increasingly visible the older it becomes. To build means to blend the lineaments of past and future in a fictitious present, an entirely drawing-like present tense inexistant outside the imagination of its

Um ihre eigene Wirklichkeit zu gewinnen, muss die Architektur eine Vergangenheit ausdrücken, die sie zugleich ersetzt, aber auch eine Zukunft, die sie mit der Zeit, je älter sie wird, desto sichtbarer macht. Bauen heißt Fluchtlinien aus Vergangenheit und Zukunft in einer fiktiven Gegenwart übereinanderzublenden, die außerhalb der Vorstellung ihres Entwerfers nicht vorkommt. In diesem Sinne ist Architektur eine vergangene Zukunft, in der herumzugehen möglich ist. Das ist das Grundprinzip des Kasperschen Projekts, das ich am besten kenne, der Neubebauung des Kaiserbadgeländes in Aachen, wo es ihm und seinen Partnern gelungen ist, ein Beispiel für das zu geben, was sie ihrer Stadt darüber hinaus zu geben gehabt hätten, wäre es ihnen nur erlaubt worden. Aber Bauen heißt auch den offenen Himmel zu bestimmen, die Bewegung der Wolken und des Lichts, Schatten schaffend, die Luft der Stadt erzeugend. Architektur fängt Regen und Wind und Schnee und Dunkelheit anders auf als die Landschaft; sie verwandelt die Verwirrung und das Wunder der Natur in Geschichte; sie schafft eine Stille, in der menschliche Stimmen Gehör finden.

Hat der Architekt Ernst Kasper das geschafft, wenn's gut ausging? Ja. Hat er's sonst versucht? Immer.

designer. In this sense, Architecture is a past future in which we are allowed to walk around. This is the underlying principle of Kasper's project that I know best, the rebuilding of the site of the Emperor's baths at Aachen where he and his associates have succeeded in achieving an example of how much more they might have given to their city if they had been allowed to do so. But building also means defining the sky above, the movement of clouds and light, creating shadows, giving the city its air. Architecture absorbs rain and wind and snow and darkness differently to landscape; architecture transforms the confusion and wonder of nature into history; it creates a quiet in which human voices will be listened to.

Has the architect Ernst Kasper succeeded in this, when things went well? Yes. Has he always been trying to achieve this? Always.

Ernst Kasper
aus einem Vortrag an der TH Hannover 1982

„Im Duft der Pflaumenblüten
Plötzlicher Sonnenaufgang –
Ah, der Bergpfad!"
Basho (1644 – 1694)

Schreiben ist nun einmal das, was ich wirklich ungern tue. Geschriebenes wirkt eben auf den Leser zweidimensional, ich meine Schlechtgeschriebenes.

Ein Haiku z. B hat auf mich eine dreidimensionale Wirkung, oft sogar eine vierdimensionale. Nun, wenn ich jetzt das, was ich mitteilen soll, in ein Haiku fassen könnte, wäre ich froh, nicht nur, weil ich mit dem Schreiben schon zu Ende wäre, es wäre eine große Leistung, ich könnte mich für einen Meister halten. Das Wesen eines Haiku habe ich zwar begriffen, es ist mir jedoch noch nicht gelungen, es auf ein Gebäude zu übertragen, aber genau das ist es, was ich eigentlich möchte, ich weiß, dass es geht. Es gibt viele Bauwerke, die es besitzen, nicht alle sind von bekannten Baumeistern. Ein Thema mit begrenzten Mitteln darzustellen ist eben nicht einfach, das Thema zu treffen noch schwieriger, und sich selbst, oder besser den Architekten in sich, im Laufe des Prozesses ganz zurückzunehmen wohl das Schwierigste.

Ernst Kasper
from a lecture at TH Hannover 1982

"The scent of the plum blossoms
Sudden sunrise –
Ah, the mountain path!"
Basho (1644-1694)

Writing is simply what I really do not like doing. The written always has a two-dimensional impact on the reader, or the poorly written at any rate.

A haiku, for example, has a three-dimensional effect on me, indeed often a four-dimensional one. Now, I would be truly glad if I were to be able to put what I want to communicate in a haiku, because then I would already have completed the writing, and it would a great achievement and I could consider myself a master. While I have understood what constitutes the essence of a haiku, I have not yet succeeded in transposing this onto a building, although that is exactly what I would actually like to do and I know it is possible. There are many edifices that have this property and not all of them were made by renowned masters of architecture. It is simply not easy to present a topic with limited means, to duly embrace that topic is even harder, and to completely background the architect within in the course of the process is probably hardest of all.

meinem Klaus für
30 Jahre langes gemeinsames
Schaffen und Leiden
ein Erinnerung Emi.
26. 08. 05

Realschule Wegberg 1965
School Wegberg 1965

Mein erstes Projekt, eine Schule für ca. 500 Schüler, auf einer Wiese am Rand einer kleinen Stadt, nichts, woran man sich anlehnen kann, nur die unsichtbare Grenze des Grundstücks, eine baumbestandene Allee und blauer Himmel. Eine Mauer, Platz für Fahrräder, ein Wohnhaus für den Hausmeister sowie eine Sporthalle und ein verdeckter Pausengang verorten das Schulgebäude, das in seiner reduzierten Form etwas den Tuchwebereien, die in der Gegend zu finden sind, ähnelt, eine Werkstatt die Schule.

My first project, a school for some 500 pupils, on a meadow at the edge of a small town. Nothing to provide inspiration apart from the invisible boundary of the plot, an avenue lined with trees and blue sky. A wall, space for bicycles, a house for the janitor, a gymnasium and a covered over walkway to be used during break time – all these anchor the school building, whose reduced form makes it resemble the cloth weaving mills located in the district. A school by way of a workshop.

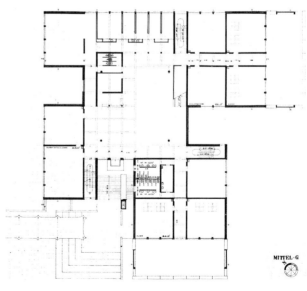

Es ist der Traum eines Architekten, aus neun Spezialisten unterschiedlicher Disziplinen ein Team zu machen, jedem gerecht zu werden und trotzdem dem Bauwerk ein unverwechselbares Gesicht zu geben.
Zu Beginn hatten wir nur das Ende bzw. für uns den Anfang eines Versorgungskanals, zum Ende schloss daran ein ganzes Heizwerk, Kälte- und Druckluftleitungen an, ergänzt durch eine Müllverbrennungsanlage.
Diese Anlage wurde vom Land NRW als „Vorbildliches Bauwerk" ausgezeichnet.

It is every architect's dream to put together a team with nine specialists from different disciplines, to do justice to the needs of each of them, and nevertheless create an edifice with an unmistakable appearance. At the beginning all we had was the end – or rather from our viewpoint the beginning of a supply channel and pipeline: at the end hooked up to it was an entire heating plant, complete with cold and compressed air pipes, supplemented by a waste incinerator.
The plant received the State of North Rhine Westphalia's prize as an "Exemplary Structure".

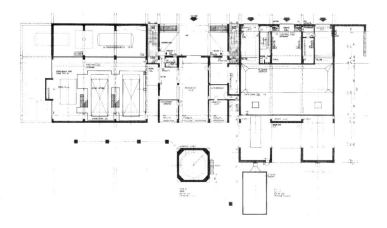

© Peter Holtfreter, Köln

Zu Anfang meiner selbstständigen Tätigkeit hatte ich mich nie richtig als Architekt betrachtet, da niemand zu mir kam in der Absicht, sein Haus mit mir zu planen, bis der Anruf kam. Mein Bauherr ist Computerfachmann. Das Raumprogramm für das Haus – säuberlich in eine Kladde eingetragen – lieferte alle notwendigen Angaben, das Grundstück war vorhanden, an einer Ausfallstraße Richtung Grenze, das drittletzte Haus, ehe der Wald anfängt. Er und sie, ein Kind sechs Jahre alt, wollten ein romantisches Haus, ein introvertiertes Haus, keine Fassade, nach außen möglichst abgeschottet, einfach.

Er am liebsten ein Atriumhaus, Platz für drei Autos und ein Boot, sein Hobby – Auto waschen, lesen, gut essen. Ihr Hobby – gut kochen und der Garten und bitte keine versetzten Ebenen. Romantik sei nicht mit Schmiedeeisen zu erzielen, warf ich ein, mit dicken Wänden, mit Licht – das sei es, was sie wollten.

Haus 1
Das Atriumhaus war ausführungsreif gezeichnet, er sagte: „Das ist es", sie: „Mich schauen immer leere Räume an", ich: „Mann, Sie haben die ganze Zeit Ihre Frau unterdrückt, es ist nur Ihr Haus." Zwei Wochen später eine Einladung zum Essen. „Eigentlich soll man sich von zwei Architekten ein Haus planen lassen, aber wir wollen nur Sie. Unser beider Wünsche sind ja nun bekannt, wären Sie bereit ein zweites Mal? Es war eben mein erster Bauherr, da muss man doch.

Haus 2
Das Dreihaushaus war ausführungsreif gezeichnet, beide einhellig zufrieden, nur die Stadt plötzlich nicht, der neue Chef wollte nur ein Haus mit „Dach" zulassen, ein richtiges Haus. Sollte man klagen? Ihr war das Haus nun auch zu groß, „können wir nicht alles kleiner machen, und das Schwimmbad muss auch nicht unbedingt sein". Es war eben mein erster Bauherr, da muss man doch. Ich wollte nun mal kein „Dach", 14 m tief, ist doch keine Scheune, kein Haus hier hat solche Proportionen, aber wenn wir es längs durchschneiden, ein Vorderhaus zur Straße, ein Hinterhaus zum Garten, beide mit Pultdach, zwischen beiden der Wohnraum, eben wie bei einem Hot Dog mit Brötchen, die Wurst zwischen zwei Brötchenhälften. Nach einer Woche schickte ich ihnen die Skizzen auf einer Rolle, 30 cm breit, 11 m lang.

At the beginning of my career as a self-employed architect I did not ever really consider myself an architect, as no one came to me with the intention of planning a house with me, until the phone suddenly rang. I at first suggested maybe the caller was mistaken, and had to ask for time to think things over, after all we had never built a house, so why did he ring me. My developer was a computer expert. The spatial program for the house – carefully entered in a folder – provided all the data I needed, the site had already been found, on a road leading out of town toward the border, the third last house before the woods started.

The couple had a child of six and wanted a romantic house, an introverted house, no façade, as closed off from the outside world as possible, simple. He most wanted a house built around an atrium, with space for up to three cars and a boat (his hobbies: washing cars, reading, good food). Her hobbies: good cooking, and the garden, and no staggered floors, please. Romanticism was not to be achieved by using wrought iron, I objected, with thick walls and with light – that was what they wanted.

House 1
The atrium house was drawn ready for building, and he said: "That's it." She said: "Empty rooms staring at me wherever I look." I said: "Husband, you have always oppressed your wife. It is only her house." Two weeks later an invitation to dinner. "Actually, people say you have to get two architects to plan your house. But we want you and you alone. You know what we both want, would you be prepared to have a second go?" It was my first developer, so I had to oblige.

House 2
The three-house house was drawn ready for building, both were agreeably happy, only the city was not, and the new boss only wanted to permit a house with a "roof", a real house. Any complaints? She now felt the house was too big as well, "can't we make everything a little smaller, and the swimming pool isn't an absolute must." It was my first developer, so I had to oblige. Now I didn't want a "roof", 14m deep, after all it wasn't to be a barn and

Haus 3

Das Zweihaushaus war ausführungsreif gezeichnet, genehmigt und fertig ausgeschrieben. Beide einhellig zufrieden und überzeugt, es sei für sie das beste Haus. Eine Woche vor Baubeginn eine Einladung zum Essen ins beste Restaurant. Nach dem dritten Gang meine Frage, was es denn jetzt für Argumente gäbe, gemeinsames Aufatmen. „Sehen Sie, der Junge ist jetzt bereits 16 Jahre und das große Haus, was ja nun, wenn es fertig ist, eigentlich unser Altenteil wird; wenn's kleiner wäre und trotzdem unser Haus." Es war eben mein erster Bauherr, der mich total betrunken nach Hause brachte, wo ich mehrmals das Bett verfehlte und die verbliebenen Wunden tagelang mit „ich hatte ein Bauherrengespräch" begründete. Jetzt wurde es wirklich schwierig, der gleiche Anspruch, aber noch kleiner. Nun, sie werden älter, der Garten wird wichtiger, das Essen, wenn wir die Küche zum Zentrum machen mit dem Wohnraum darüber, als Palais sozusagen, alles andere wie Remisen oder Vorbauten schützend darumlegen, so müsste es gehen, und da kein Platz mehr für ein Badehaus ist, setzen wir die Badewanne in den Wohnraum, zum Entspannen, zum Lesen – beide waren begeistert, sie hätten nicht gedacht – ich hätte ihre Wünsche wieder voll getroffen.

Haus 4

Das Einhaushaus war ausführungsreif gezeichnet, genehmigt und ausgeschrieben, nur keiner weiß genau warum, es war um ein Drittel zu teuer. Zwölf Jahre waren vergangen – ich habe keinen Bauherrn mehr – er keinen Architekten. Sie haben sich jetzt ein Haus ersteigert, zwei Jahre alt, weit außerhalb, eine Kreuzung aus Pudel und Dackel.

no house here had such proportions, but if we cut it down the middle lengthwise, a front building facing the road, a rear building opening onto the garden, both of them with a roof sloping to one side, a living room between the two, like a hot dog between the two bun halves. After a week I had the sketches ready to send them on a roll, 30cm wide, 11m long.

House 3

The two-house house was drawn ready for building, had been approved and tenders made. Both sides seemed agreeably satisfied and convinced that it was the best house for them. A week before construction work was to start I received a dinner invite, the best restaurant in town. After the third course I asked what the arguments now were, and the two breathed a sigh of relief. "Well you see, our boy's now 16 and the large house, which will now, once it's finished, be the place where we live when we're old; if it were smaller it would still be our house." It was my first developer who got me home completely drunk, I missed the bed a few times trying to climb onto it, and justified the wounds left on my legs for days afterwards by saying 'talked with my developer'. Now things became really difficult, the same standards required, but still smaller. And they became older, the garden became more important, eating too, how about making the kitchen the center of things, with the living room over it, like a palace, everything else like coach-houses or protective outbuildings, surely it must work out, and since there was no space for a bathhouse left we would put the tub in the living room, for relaxation and reading – both were captivated by the idea, they had never imagined that – yes, I had once again understood their wishes perfectly.

House 4

The one-house house was drawn ready for building, had been approved and tenders made, only no one really knows why it was one third more expensive. 12 years had passed – I no longer have a developer – and he no longer has an architect. They have now bought a house by auction, two years old, a long way out, a cross between a poodle and a dachshund.

Wohnhaus Funke Fassung 1
Funke Residence Version 1

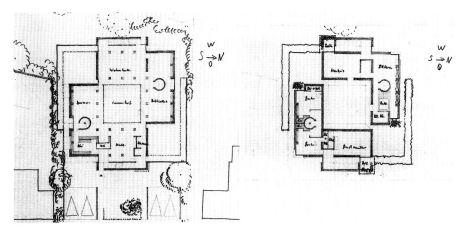

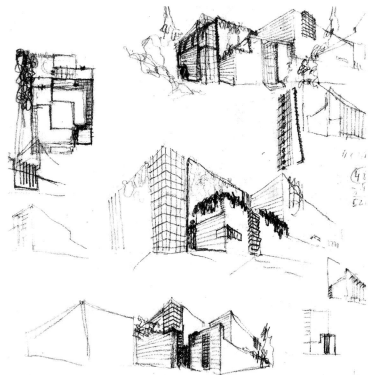

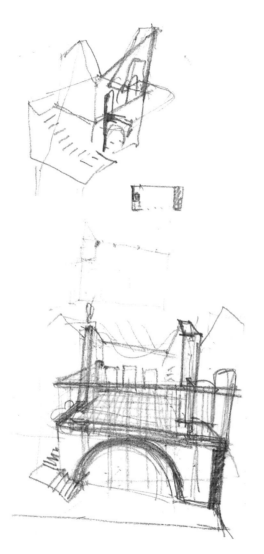

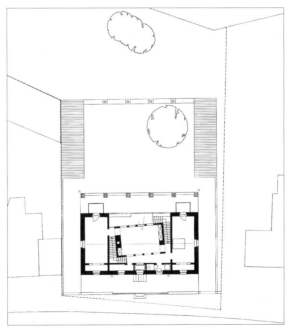

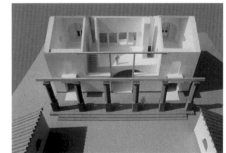

Kunstpalast Düsseldorf 1985
"Art Palace" in Düsseldorf 1985

Zum Ehrenhof steht die Fassade schon. Rotunde und Patio nutzen wir als Orte der Erinnerung, nur die alten Hallen ersetzen wir durch neue, so, dass die Tradition der Ausstellung gewahrt bleibt. Die Musik bekommt auch ein Haus.

The façade facing Ehrenhof already exists. We use the rotunda and the patio as spaces for remembrance, replacing only the old halls with new ones, such that the tradition of the exhibition is preserved. Music also receives a roof over its head.

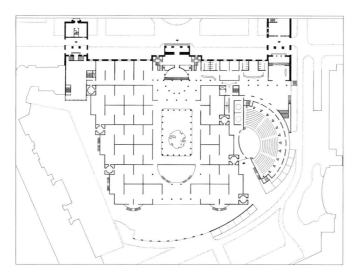

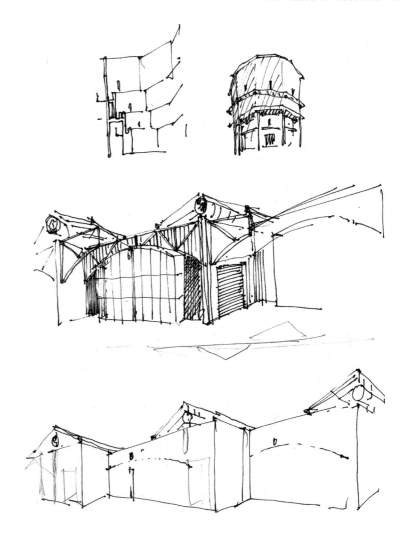

Kunstpalast Düsseldorf 1976
"Art Palace" in Düsseldorf 1976

Berufsschulen Kempen / Viersen 1977
Vocational colleges in Kempen / Viersen 1977

Diese Schulen gleichen einer Kette mit Anhängern. Die Anhänger sind die Fachabteilungen, die Kette die Klassenräume, die von Jahr zu Jahr unterschiedlich zugewiesen werden, mal mehr den Maurern oder den Kfz-Technikern, den Bäckern oder Frisören. Man kann sie auch sehen wie mehrere Schulen, die sich einander an den Händen halten. Beide Schulen dienten dem neu aufkommenden Thema „Schule in der Schule" als Vorbild. Städtebaulich bilden sie jeweils Rand und Grenze einer ausufernden Bebauung. Industrielle Bauten der Region waren vertraute Vorbilder.

These colleges resemble chains with pendants. The pendants are the specialist departments, the chain the classrooms, which are allocated differently from year to year, sometimes more going to the bricklayers or the car mechanics, the bakers or the hairdressers. Alternately, you can view them as several schools holding each other by the hand. Both colleges were inspired by the recent concept of "a school within a school". In terms of urban planning, they form the edge and border of a sprawling development. Industrial buildings in the region served as familiar models.

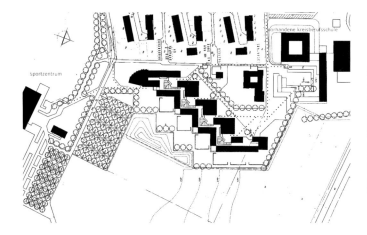

Berufsschulen Kempen / Viersen 1977
Vocational colleges in Kempen / Viersen 1977

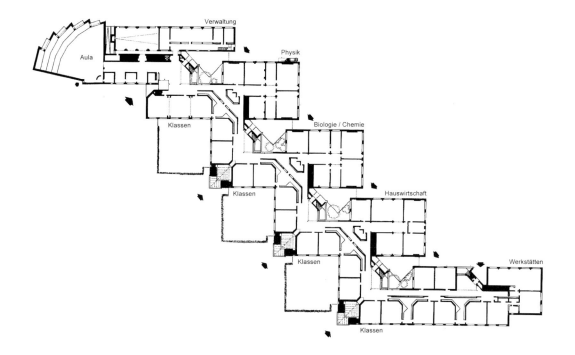

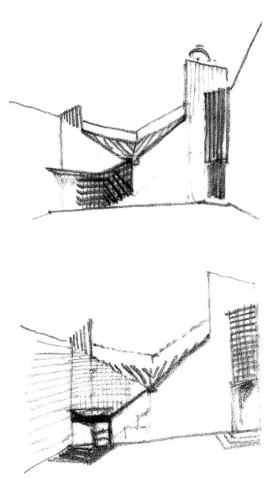

Berufsschulen Kempen / Viersen 1977
Vocational colleges in Kempen / Viersen 1977

44

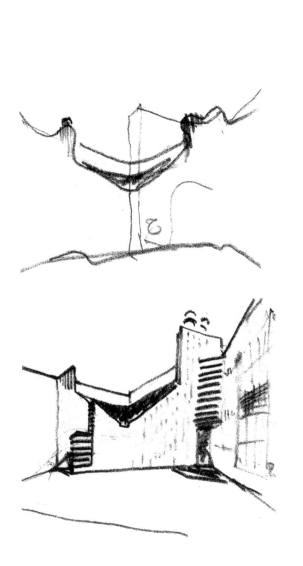

Sanierung Schnellengasse Eschweiler 1978
Redevelopment Schnellengasse in Eschweiler 1978

Ein Haus stand. Zwei Fassaden anderer Häuser waren noch intakt. Gesucht war ein Gesamtkonzept, Wohnungen und Läden, größere Läden. Wir haben die Gesamtfläche aus ihrem Schwerpunkt heraus geordnet mit Hilfe dreier Höfe, keine künstliche Hinterhofidylle, überall Fassade, überall Außenraum. Es sollte etwas Französisches haben.

One house was still standing. The façades of two other houses were still intact. The aim was to find a general concept embracing apartments, shops and larger stores. We structured the composition of the whole area around a focal point created from three courtyards. No attempt was made to create a backyard idyll, there is a dominance of façade and the outdoors.
It was to have a French flair.

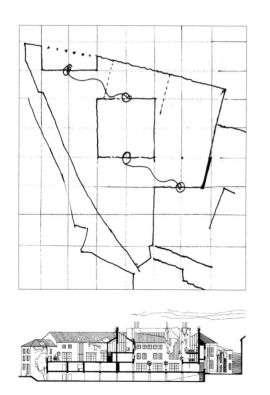

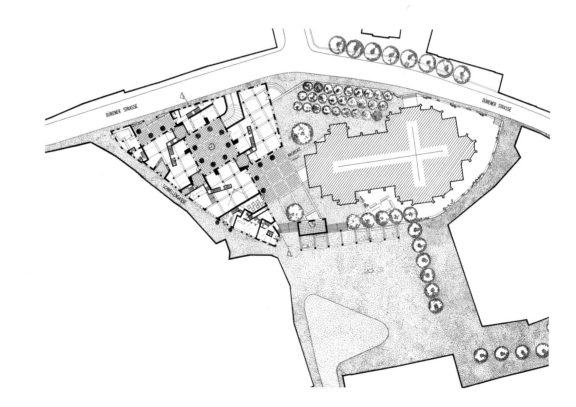

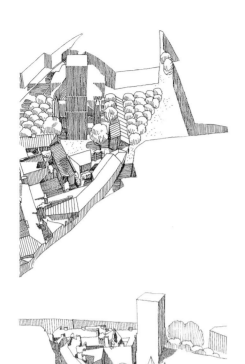

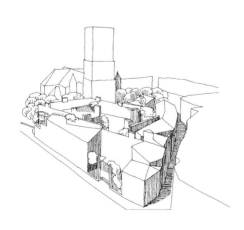

Stiftisch-Humanistisches Gymnasium Mönchengladbach 1978
High School in Mönchengladbach 1978

Das Stiftisch-Humanistische Gymnasium in Mönchengladbach (Altsprachlich, Latein und Griechisch) ist eine Schule alter Tradition. Nicht mehr funktionsfähig, wurde es abgebrochen und von uns durch einen Neubau ersetzt. Dieser liegt am Rande einer Endmoräne, in einer Reihe mit der Stiftskirche, dem ehemaligen Stift, in dem heute das Rathaus ist, und dem bekannten Museum von Hans Hollein. Die Schule fasst ca. 500 Schüler. Es war gewünscht, die Wegeführung des Museums durch das Schulgelände hindurchzuleiten, ferner war erwünscht, eine 500 Jahre alte Ulme zu erhalten. Zu Beginn der Planung stand die Ulme noch, als wir mit dem Bau begannen, war sie durch eine Pilzkrankheit, die damals alle Ulmen erfasste, abgestorben. Das Grundstück war sehr beengt.
Der Name der Schule – Stiftisches Gymnasium – gab den Anstoß, diese drei Hofformen zu wählen. Die Schule ist über einer Tiefgarage errichtet, die einzelnen Hofgebäude sind unterirdisch miteinander verbunden. Die Schüler der einzelnen Jahrgangsstufen können auf ihrer jeweiligen Ebene gleich ins Freie. Ein öffentlicher Weg läuft vom Museum her über das Schulgebäude.

The Stiftisch-Humanistische Gymnasium in Mönchengladbach (high school teaching the classics, namely Latin and Greek) is a college in an old tradition. No longer functional, the old building had to be torn down and our task was to design a replacement. The building is situated on the edge of the end of a moraine, in the same line as the Stiftskirche, the former monastic foundation (the "Stift"), which now houses the town hall, and the well-known museum created by Hans Hollein. The school can take up to 500 pupils. The client wanted to have the paths for the museum run across the school grounds and for a 500-year-old elm to be left standing. When we started devising our plans, the elm tree was still standing, but once building work began, it had fallen victim to a fungus which was attacking many elm trees at the time. The site was very confined. The school's name, "Stiftisches Gymnasium" or "Cloister Foundation High School" was the reason why we chose these three courtyard shapes. The school was to be located over an underground and the individual courtyard buildings are linked underground. The pupils in the individual grades can simply step outdoors at their respective level. A public footpath leads from the museum over to the school building.

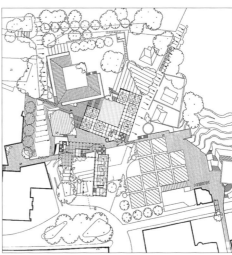

Stiftisch-Humanistisches Gymnasium Mönchengladbach 1978
High School in Mönchengladbach 1978

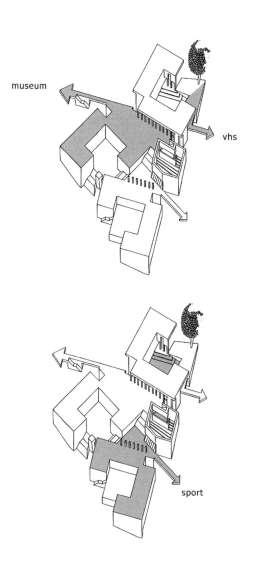

museum

vhs

sport

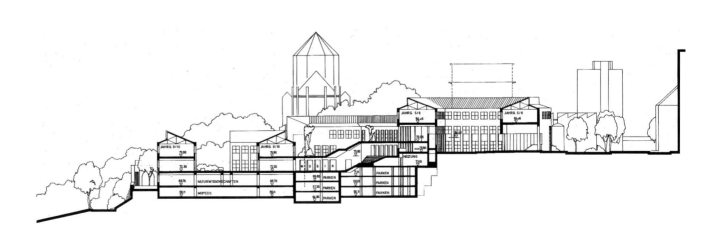

Museum Ludwig Aachen 1979
Museum Ludwig in Aachen 1979

Was ist ein Museum, warum geht man dahin? Mir fiel eine Geschichte ein, die Erwin Heerich nach seiner Ägyptenreise erzählte, die „Totenstadt": Feiertags oder auch so geht man zur Totenstadt, außerhalb der Mauer, sitzt in Häusern, die aussehen wie Häuser für Lebende, die aber die Häuser der Toten sind, man isst von dem Mitgebrachten und erinnert sich der Toten, lernt aus der Vergangenheit. Ein Museum als „Totenstadt", keine Fabrikhalle, kein Mausoleum, Häuser für Kunstwerke, Häuser, in die man reingehen kann, um die man herumlaufen kann, durch die man hindurchgehen kann, eine kleine Stadt für die Kunst, ein durchlässiges Gebilde zwischen Allee und Park, der Kontext zur umgebenden Bebauung wäre damit auch gewahrt. Unser erstes Konzept war, mehrere Villen vorzusehen, die miteinander verbunden, jede von einem anderen bekannten Architekten ausgeführt werden sollten. Das Programm hatte jedoch einen größeren Umfang, als wir anfangs dachten, auch passte die zeitgenössische Kunst nicht in das Konzept der Villen. So haben wir uns bei der Kunst vor 1900 für die „Kabinette", und bei der nach 1900 für die „Lofts" entschieden, und da die meisten Werke der Sammlung so was „Voyeuristisches" hatten, eigneten sich die Lofts sehr gut für unsere Durchgangsstraßen, auf denen man ja, quasi wie durch ein Schlüsselloch, ab und zu in die Ausstellungsräume hätte schauen können.

What is a museum and why do you go there. A story occurred to me that Erwin Heerich narrated after a trip to Egypt, the "City of the Dead": on holidays people go to the City of the Dead, or on other days, too – outside the walls, sit in houses that look like houses for the living but which are in fact houses for the dead; they eat what they took along with them and remember the dead, learning from the past. A museum as a "City of the Dead", not a factory hall, not a mausoleum, houses for artworks, houses which you enter, walk around in, walk through, a small town for art, a permeable structure between an avenue and a park, thus preserving the context of the surrounding buildings. Our first concept envisaged several villas linked to one another, each of them to be designed by a different renowned architect. The program turned out to be greater in scope than we had originally thought, and contemporary art did not sit pretty with the concept of the villas. We therefore chose "cabinets" for art prior to 1900 and "lofts" for the art after that date, and since most of the works in the collection had something "voyeuristic" about them, lofts were highly suitable for our thoroughfares, from which, almost as if through key holes, you can now and then glimpse into the exhibition rooms.

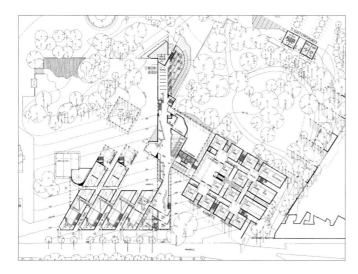

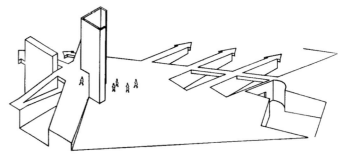

Rathaus Dortmund 1980
Town Hall in Dortmund 1980

Eine symbolische Lösung, der Ratssaal als Teil der Bürgerhalle gemäß unserer demokratischen Verfassung. Die Dimension der Bürgerhalle ist als Patio fortgesetzt, als Amtshof und als Ruhehof. Der Marktplatz ist durch die Rathausfassade und Marktarkaden gefasst. Im Zusammenhang mit der alten Stadthausfassade maß- und raumbildende Elemente.

A symbolic solution, the Council Chambers as part of the Civic Hall and in keeping with our democratic constitution. The dimensions of the Civic Hall are also adopted for the patio, for the Amtshof (Official Courtyard) and for the Ruhehof (Contemplation Courtyard). The Town Hall's façade and market arcades bracket the market square. Together with the old Stadthaus façade they define the proportions and serve as spatial elements.

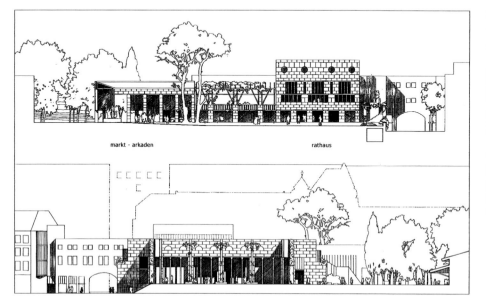

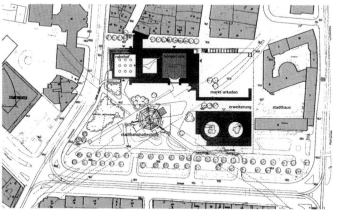

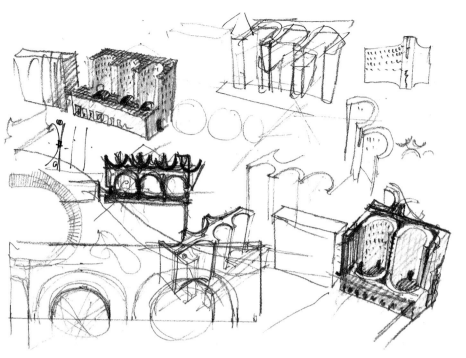

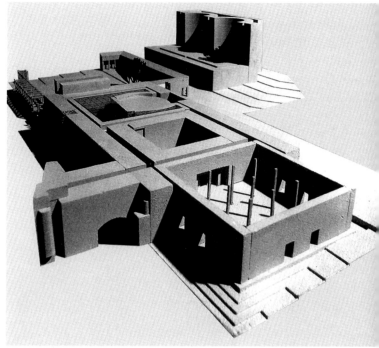

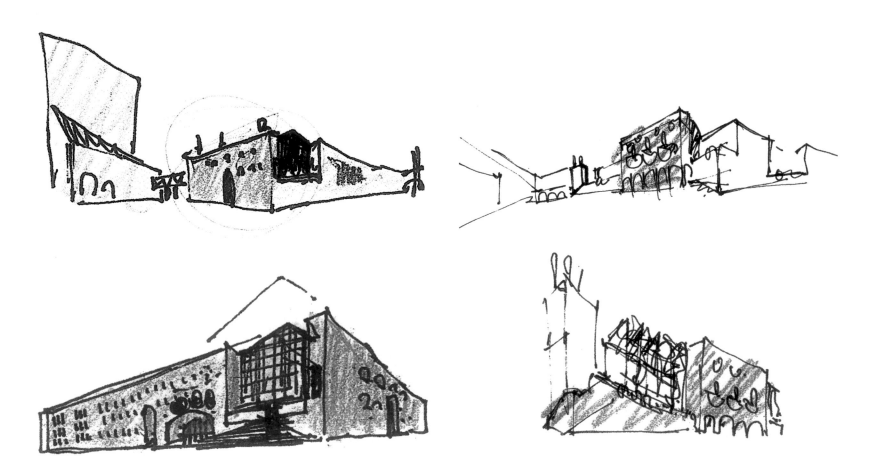

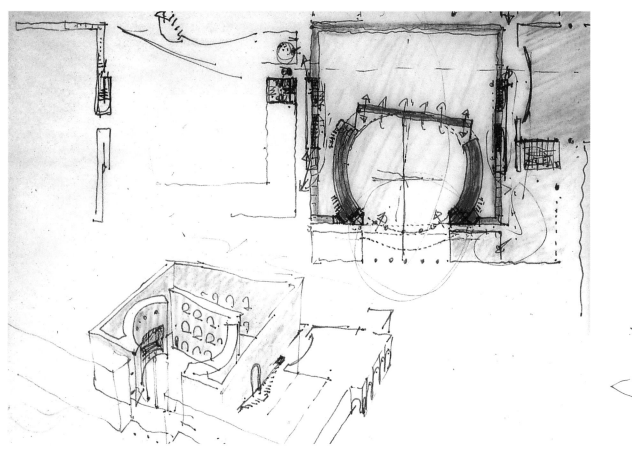

Diesen Wettbewerb haben wir einfach so begonnen. Das städtebauliche Konzept war schon in den ersten Tagen geklärt. Wir wollten nicht über fünf Geschosse gehen, zum Straßenbereich eine Blockrandbebauung machen und im Grünbereich in einer großen geschwungenen Form auf das in Bau befindliche Freizeitzentrum reagieren. Die geforderten Sicherheitskriterien zwangen zur Geschlossenheit der Anlage. Soweit waren wir zwar, nur hatte alles noch keine Seele, es war noch kein Justizgebäude, aber was ist das? Beim Lesen des Programms war mir von Anfang an die Anwaltshalle aufgefallen, vielleicht auch, weil wir nicht wussten, was das war. Ist nicht vor Gericht der Angeklagte oft sprachlos, spricht nicht der Anwalt für ihn, ist sein Mentor? Bei der Besichtigung des Aachener Amtsgerichtes erwies sich diese Raumzone lediglich als simpler Garderobenraum, irgendwo gelegen. Keiner maß ihr eine besondere Bedeutung bei. Wir kamen nicht weiter. In meiner Verzweiflung fuhr ich nach Brüssel und besuchte dieses Ungetüm von Justizpalast. Siehe, in seiner Mitte, unter dieser riesigen Kuppel ein großer Raum, einsehbar von allen internen Hauptwegen, in Nischen an Tischen sitzend, Anwälte mit ihren Klienten. Die räumlichen Dimensionen zwar gigantisch,

We started preparing our competition entry without much thought. The concept as regards urban planning took only a few days to get ready. We wanted a max. five stories building flush with the sidewalks on the sides facing roads, and a large curved shape toward the green-belt that responded to the leisure time center that was under construction. The security standards required meant the structure had top be closed off. So far so good, but we had a building without a soul, it was not yet a building for the courts, but what is? When I read the brief I had immediately noticed the hall for attorneys, perhaps also because we did not know what it was. On visiting the Aachen District Court we established that this zone was simply a glorified cloakroom, located somewhere or other. No one attached any importance to it. We were not getting any further. In desperation, I traveled to Brussels and visited that monster of a Palace of Justice. And what do you now, at its heart, beneath the huge dome, there was a large room, visible from all the main internal arteries, and there, in niches sat attorneys talking with their clients. The spatial dimensions were gigantic, but it exuded a sense

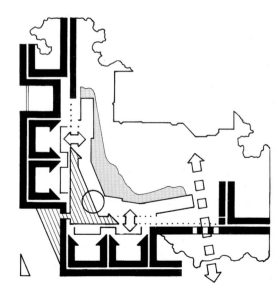

doch alles strahlte Ruhe, Gelassenheit und Vertrauen aus und die Würde war mit der Heiterkeit im Gleichgewicht. Also doch die Anwaltshalle, sagte ich mir, genauso, nur nicht von gleicher Gestalt, doch von gleicher Ausstrahlung, und fuhr zufrieden heim. Wir legten also unsere Anwaltshalle gleich nahe dem Eingang in den Winkel beider Erschließungsstraßen, als einsehbare und betretbare Zone, die von den Verkehrswegen lediglich tangiert wird, unterteilt in Lobby, Arbeitszone und Garderobe, mit Durchblick und Ausblick auf den Grünbereich. Diese Zone bildet in der Gesamtarchitektur den Bereich, wo die strenge Form des Bauwerks mehrfach aufgebrochen wird, dort werden zu strengen baulichen Regeln Kontraste so gesetzt, dass alles in der Schwebe ist, das Gefüge in Frage gestellt und das Freie in die Ordnung eingebunden wird. Wir meinen, mit diesen architektonischen Mitteln eine Atmosphäre zu erreichen, die vielleicht ein neues Justizgebäude ausmacht, eine Atmosphäre, wo sich Heiterkeit und Würde die Waage halten.

of calm, of leisure, and of trust, with human dignity before the law harmonizing with cheerfulness. So we need a hall for attorneys after all, I told myself, exactly like this one, not shaped like it but exuding the same feel, and drove home happy. So we placed our hall for attorneys close to the entrance in the angle between the two access roads, a visible and easily reached zone merely touched on by the access routes, sub-divided into a lobby, work zones and cloakroom, with views inward and a view out over the green-belt. In the overall architecture, the zone forms the area where the stringent shape of the edifice is abandoned in several ways, contrasts to the strict building regulations set in such a manner that everything seems to be undecided, as if the edifice itself were cast into question, with liberty being inserted into order and vice versa. We are of the opinion that these architectural means foster an atmosphere which perhaps characterizes a new form of court complex, an atmosphere in which cheerfulness and dignity go hand in hand.

Justizbehörden Dortmund 1980
Court Building in Dortmund 1980

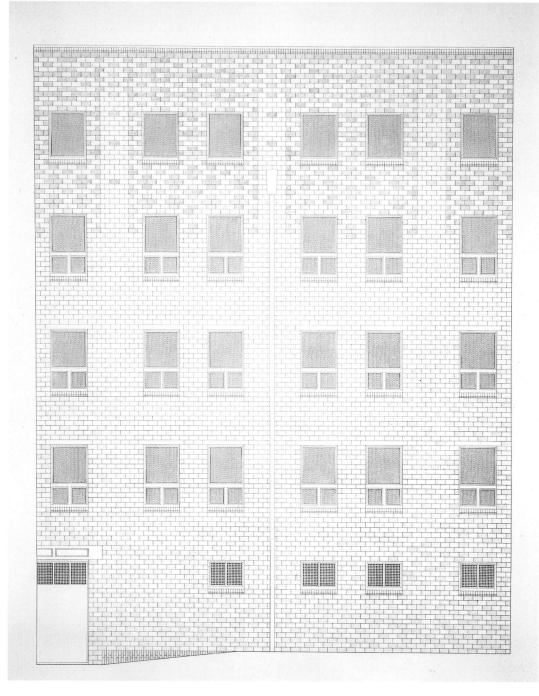

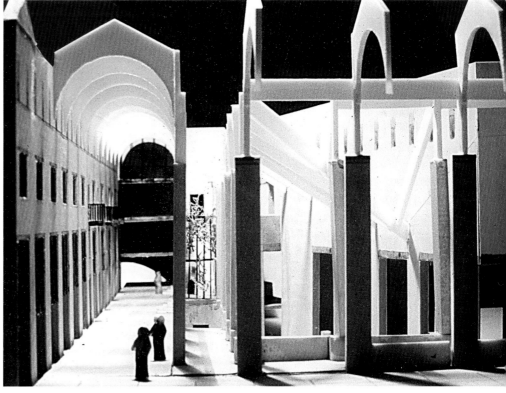

Jürgen Rektorwind Werkszenen

Rathaus und Pfarrzentrum Wittlich 1984
Town Hall and Parrish Center in Wittlich 1984

Wir haben nur einen Straßenraum, also keine Distanz für eine Fassade, die wir ja auch gar nicht wollten, es ist eine Nordseite, kein Licht, kein Schatten, um eine Fassade zu gestalten, außerdem müssen wir es erreichen, mit dem Betreten des Straßenraumes das Gefühl zu vermitteln, bereits im Rathaus zu stehen, ganz plötzlich muss man im Rathaus stehen. Um das zu erreichen, dürfen wir keine Fassade machen, die als solche ja auch nur eine Bildhaftigkeit von Rathaus darstellt, man muss drinnen sein, und dazu müssen wir es erst gar nicht als Rathaus bekleiden, wir zeigen gleich das Innere, und da wir die Nordseite haben, müssen wir Licht auf die Wände bringen, und das erreichen wir durch einen Trick, indem wir mit einem bestimmten Abstand ein Vordach davor setzen, und zwar so, dass man, gleich wo man steht, nur unter das Dach schauen kann, damit ist man gefühlsmäßig im Gebäude, und der Lichtschlitz macht die Wände heller als ohne Vordach, erstens wegen der Kontraste Dachuntersicht zu Wand, zweitens aus Gründen der Reflexion. Das war unsere Lösung für ein Rathaus, das seine Arme ausbreitet, das mit der Sichtbarmachung von Typologien von Ratssaal und Verwaltung, also von Legislative und Exekutive, sich als solches auch darstellt.

At street level we lack the space needed for a façade, although this was not considered desirable since the street faces north, and there would be no light or shadow to modulate a façade. Moreover, we need to convey the feeling when you stand on the street of already being inside the Town Hall, of being immediately transported inside it. We could not use a façade – basically a visual symbol of the Town Hall – to achieve this sensation. Nor, indeed do we need to present the exterior as a Town Hall but immediately show the interior, and as this is the North side we need to direct light onto the walls. We achieve that using the following device: we installed a canopy at a certain distance in such a manner that regardless of where you stand you can only look below it. This creates the impression of being inside the building, and the light slit makes the walls lighter than if there were no canopy firstly because of the contrasts between the view below the canopy and the wall, and secondly because reflection is created. This was our solution for a Town Hall that extends its arms outwards. The building presents itself as a Town Hall by rendering the Council Chambers and Administration highly visible – after all, the two represent the legislative and executive functions.

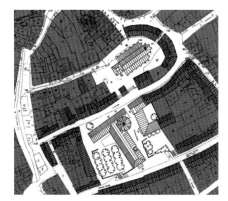
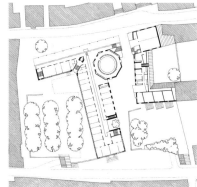

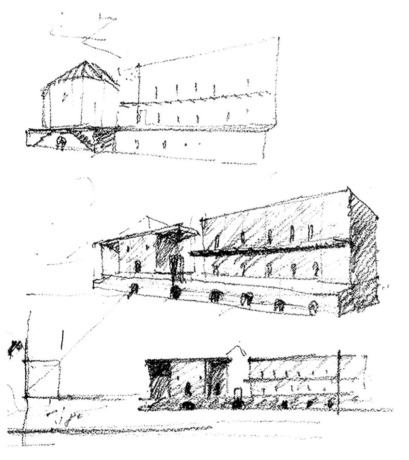

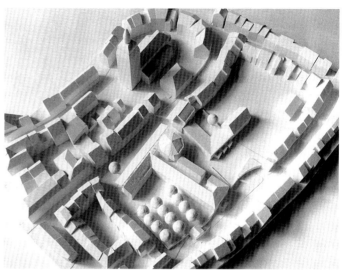

Museum und Bibliothek Münster 1985
Municipal Museum and Library in Münster 1985

Zwischen St. Lamberti und Kiffe Pavillon längs der Außenkrümmung des Alten Steinwegs, einer ehemaligen Reichsstraße, lagen wie aufgereiht einst Palais des Münsteraner Geldadels. Genau dieses Bild, auch ähnlich einer Rissstruktur bei Außenseiten von Krümmungen, war uns Anlass für Position, Form und Maß der Bauelemente.

Between St. Lamberti and the Kiffe Pavilion along the curved line of Alter Steinweg, which was once an Imperial Road, the fine town houses of the moneyed gentry of Münster stood like beads on a chain. This was exactly the image, including the ruptured structure with outer edges that curved and bended, that we focused on when defining the position, shape and proportions of the building elements.

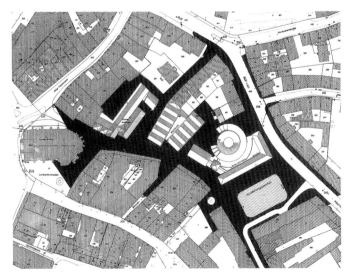

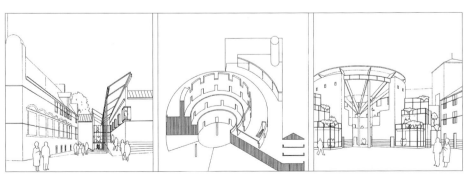

Fortbildungszentrum Finanzverwaltung Münster, NRW 1985
North Rhine Westphalian Tax Administration, boarding college for further training in Münster 1985

Eingebettet in die Lichtung eines Hauwaldes, am Rande weit gestreuter Einfamilienhäuser, ein Elysium, ein Ort, an dem man sich weit weg fühlen kann, ein Ort für eine Gemeinschaft von Lernenden auf Zeit.

Embedded in the main clearing of the wooded grounds, with generously spaced detached houses on the periphery; it is a haven, a place where you can feel far removed from everything, a place for a community of people undergoing temporary instruction.

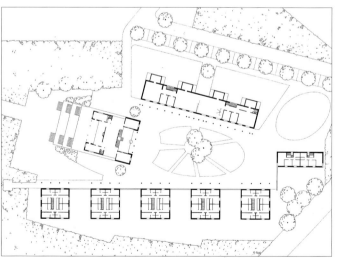

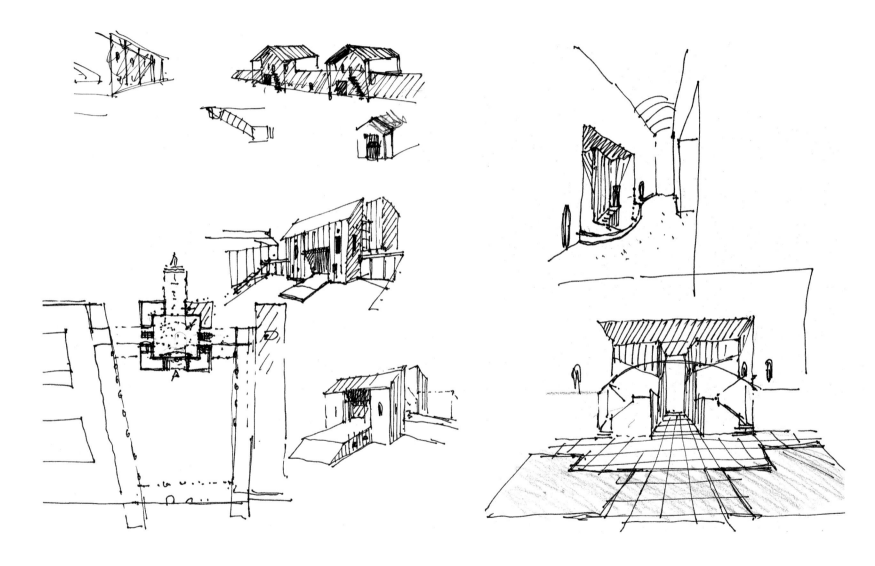

Goethe-Institut München 1986
Goethe Institute in Munich 1986

Die Außenkanten des Blocks sind festgeschrieben. Nur innen haben wir also Freiheit, ein Thema zu finden und reden, da es ein Park werden soll, ständig über Goethes Reise nach Italien. Geblieben ist das Oval, das sich nach außen durchdrückt, ein Motiv der Unendlichkeit, von hoher Gestalt, zur schnellen Straße hin wird das im Einschnitt durchscheinende Innere in die Länge gezogen, gleich einer Anamorphose.

The outer edges of the block were defined and could not be altered. In other words, we only had the freedom to find a theme for the interior and, since the idea was to create a park, constantly refer to Goethe's trip to Italy. What has remained is an oval that pushes its way onto the outside, a motif for infinity, striking and high – on the side facing the highway, the interior, visible within the cut-out section, is given greater length rather than height, essentially an anamorphic change.

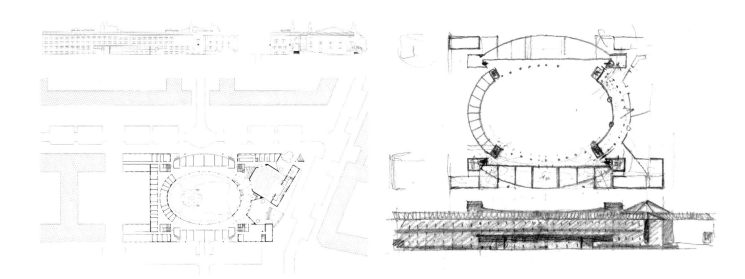

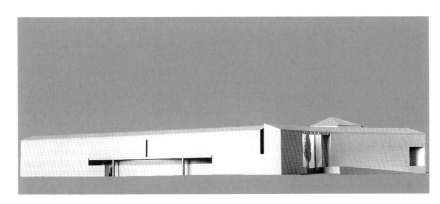

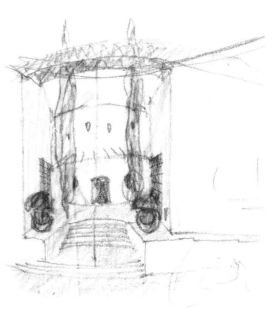

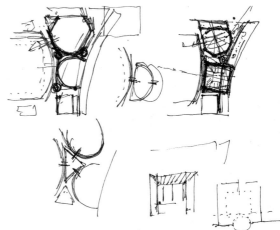

Marienplatz München 1986
Marienplatz in Munich 1986

Die ehemalige Bebauung, sowie die damit nicht vorhandenen Fassaden für einen entsprechenden Platz, außer denen an der Dienerstraße, veranlassen uns, einen Block vorzuschlagen, der mit anderen Mitteln, also nur baulichen, erstellt werden kann. Wir meinen die, innerhalb der belebten Abfolge von Straßen, Straßenräumen und Plätzen, gelegenen meditativen Räume wie „Frauenkirche" und „Alter Hof" um einen weiteren, den „Marienhof" ergänzen zu müssen, um so ein gewisses Gleichgewicht im öffentlichen Bereich wieder herzustellen. Dabei ist uns der Kontrast wichtiger als ein verspielter Zwischenbereich, eine Regeneration der Sinne und des Sinnlichen, die Abgrenzung wichtiger als weiche Übergänge. In dem Geviert von 90 m x 90 m stehen 132 Linden auf einem Schotterrasen. Sie haben irgendwann die Höhe der umliegenden Trafen, sie bewegen sich gleichmäßig im Wind, sie rauschen, sie duften während der Blütezeit, sie zeigen die Jahreszeiten an, sie bilden einen meditativen Raum großer Schönheit. Die Umfassungen nehmen, entsprechend der Innen- oder Außenseite, die gewünschten Funktionen auf, wie U-Bahn-Ausgänge, Taxiwarteplätze, ein Wintergarten, wind- und wettergeschützte Sitzplätze …

Das Geviert bleibt frei von jeder Nutzung, nur 132 Linden. Dies ist uns sehr wichtig, den Randbereich kann man auch anders formulieren, etwas offener oder noch mehr geschlossen, oder andere Materialien, er soll jedoch von großer Einfachheit sein und nur die Variation eines Prinzips, das gleichsam der inneren wie der äußeren Nutzung entgegenkommt.

The former buildings, as well as the non-existing façades for a corresponding square, with the exception of those on Dienerstrasse, prompted us to propose a block that could be created using different means, in other words only by construction. We believe it necessary to extend the meditative spaces such as the "Frauenkirche" and the "Alter Hof" located within the thriving sequences of roads, street spaces, and plazas to include the "Marienhof" in order to regain a certain balance within the public space. In this regard, we have prioritized contrast rather than some ornate interface, fostering the regeneration of the senses and the sensuous, with demarcation more important than soft transitions. In the square sized 90m x 90m there are 132 linden trees on gravel terraces. At some point they have the same height as the surrounding eaves, move regularly in the wind, rustle, are fragrant when in blossom, indicate the seasons, form a meditative space that if very beautiful. The frame, in line with the inside or outside, houses the required functions, such as subway entrances, taxibays, a wintergarden, seats protected from the wind and weather …

The square has no use other than to support the 132 linden trees. We feel this is very important, the outer margins can be construed differently, rendered somewhat more open or closed, or other materials used for them, but they must be of the utmost simplicity and provide at most a variation on a principle that fosters both inner and outer uses.

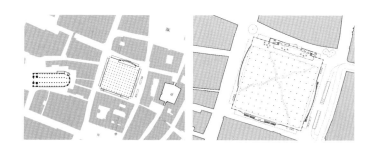

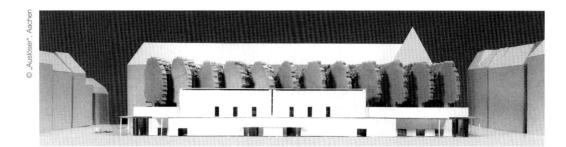

Kulturhaus am Hexenturm Jülich 1987
Library and town museum in Jülich 1987

Jülich, eine Renaissance-Festungsstadt, im Zweiten Weltkrieg sehr zerstört, ist noch im Besitz eines mittelalterlichen Stadttores, dem so genannten Hexenturm. Hier galt es, auf freiem Grund, dem Tor ein Gebäude hinzuzufügen, genutzt als Bibliothek, und verbunden mit dem Turm als Museum für Stadtgeschichte. Der vorgelagerte große Platz, Busbahnhof und Parkplatz zugleich, sollte mit dieser Maßnahme ein Gesicht zur Innenstadt erhalten. Dieses neue Gebäude ringt um das richtige Maß zum Turm, beginnt scheinbar als Mauer, um zum Ende hin – dem Platz im Wesentlichen zugewandt – als Fassade zur erscheinen. Die eingelassenen Marmorprismen sollen die Gebäudehaut weit in den Platzraum hinein wirken lassen.

Jülich, a Renaissance fortress town that suffered much damage in World War II, has an intact Medieval entrance to the town known as the Hexenturm (Witches' Tower). The idea was to complement the Tower with a building on nearby vacant ground. This new building accommodating a library is connected to the Tower, which serves as a local history museum. One objective in doing this was to lend a face to that side of the large square (which doubles as bus station and car park) facing the downtown area. This new building twists itself upward to achieve the right scale to match the Tower. Initially it appears as a wall before finally – largely facing the square – presenting itself as a façade. The inset marble prisms are designed to extend the impact of the building's skin far into the space taken up by the square.

Lukas Roth, Köln

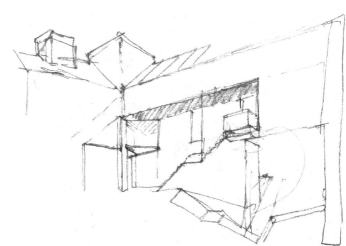

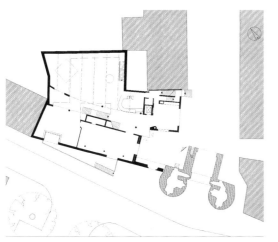

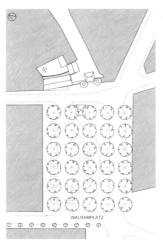

WALRAMPLATZ

Kulturhaus am Hexenturm Jülich 1987
Library and town museum in Jülich 1987

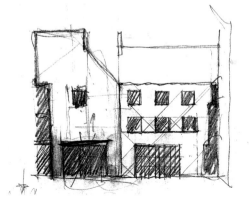

Haus der Geschichte Bonn 1987
Hall of History in Bonn 1987

Der Weg ist ein Partner der Zeit.
Das Problem war nie der Einstieg, sondern der Ausstieg.

The path is the partner of time.
The problem was not the beginning but the end.

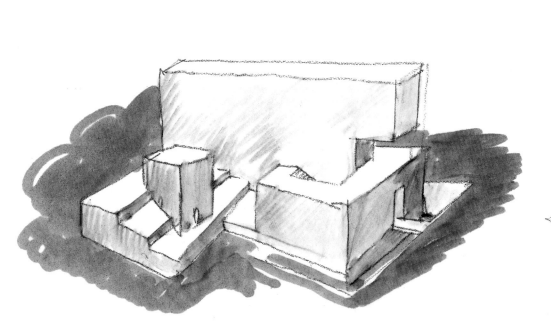

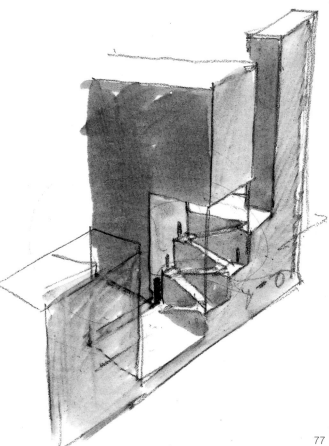

Bibliothek TU Berlin 1987
Library in Berlin 1987

Die Bibliothek dient der Technischen Universität wie der Hochschule der Künste als Hort der Bücher. Eine Landmarke des Viertels am Rande des Tiergartens. Die getreppten Terrassen, die Lesesäle sind dem ehemaligen Hippodrom zugewandt.

Both the Technical University and the Art Academy store their books in the library. A landmark for the quarter on the periphery of the Tiergarten. The staggered terraces and reading rooms face the former Hippodrome.

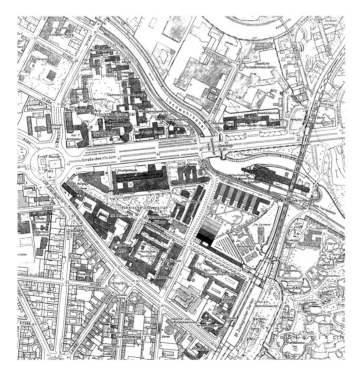
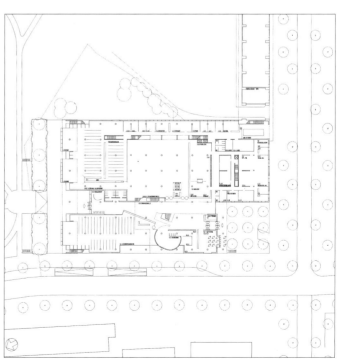

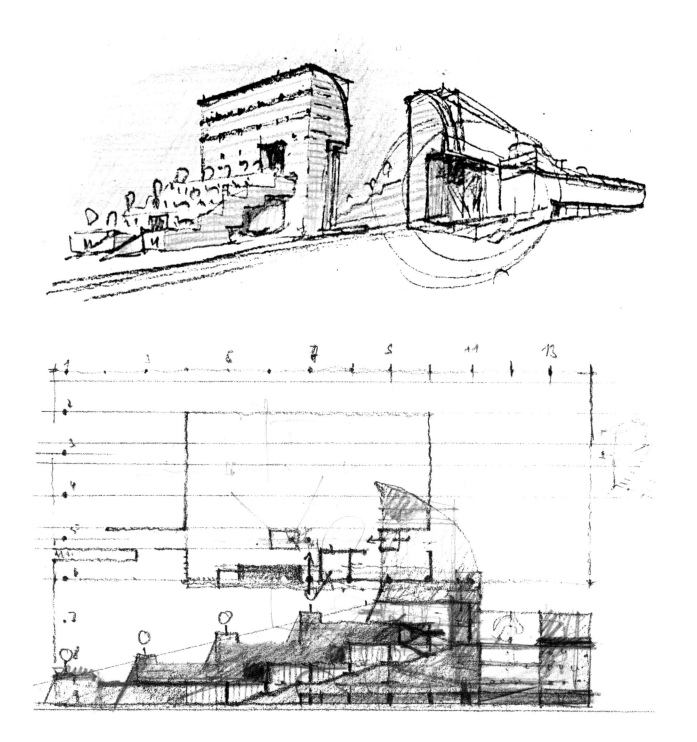

Museum für Glasmalerei Linnich 1989
Museum for Painted Glass in Linnich 1989

Eine ehemalige Wassermühle am Rand und Wall der kleinen Stadt, wird ausgebaut und erweitert zu einem Museum für Glasbilder, dem ersten Museum für Glasbilder in Deutschland. Dieser Ort ist sowohl Aufgang zu den Wallanlagen, Zugang zum Museum als auch Zugang zu einem Wegesystem längs des Mühlenbaches, daher das „Flic-Flac"-Prinzip. Die möglichst sprossenfreie Verglasung zur Darbietung der unterschiedlichen Glasbilder führt im Vergleich zum Vorhandenen zu unterschiedlich großen Maßstäben.

The former mill on the outskirts of the small town next to the old town walls is being expanded and extended to house a Museum for Painted Glass, the first museum of its kind in Germany. The location is both the beginning of the staircase up the town walls, entrance to the museum, and the beginning of the system of paths leading along the Mühlenbach River, which explains the "flic-flac" principle. Compared with the existing building, the glass front has been kept as uncluttered by sash bars as possible to enhance the presentation of the different glass pictures, creating new, differently sized proportions.

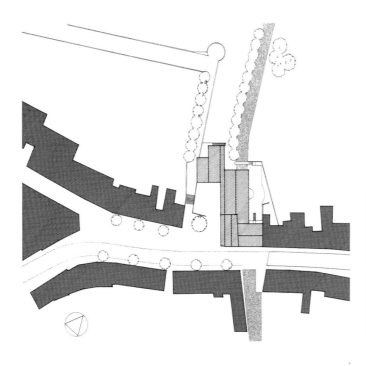

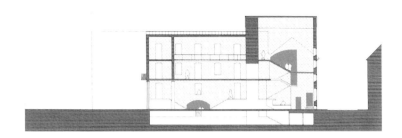

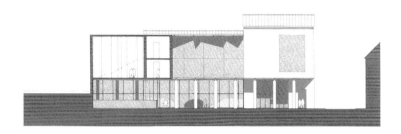

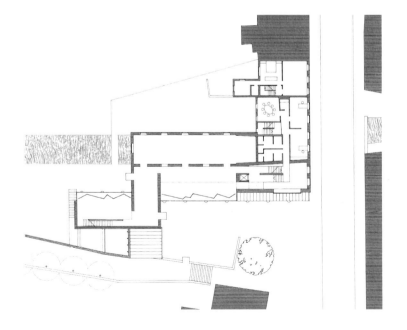

Sporthalle Arndt-Gymnasium Krefeld 1989
Sports Hall, Arndt High School in Krefeld 1989

Eine Sporthalle mit Tribünen in die Lücke eingefügt, auch als Aula genutzt, ebenso zusätzliche Klassenräume schreiben die Straßenzeile einfach weiter.

A sports hall with stands for seated viewers inserted into the gap; it can double up as a auditorium or as additional class rooms, and simply continues the line of the street.

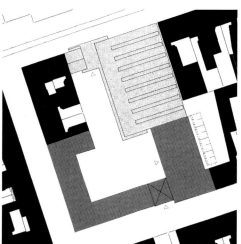

© Marcus Schwier, Düsseldorf

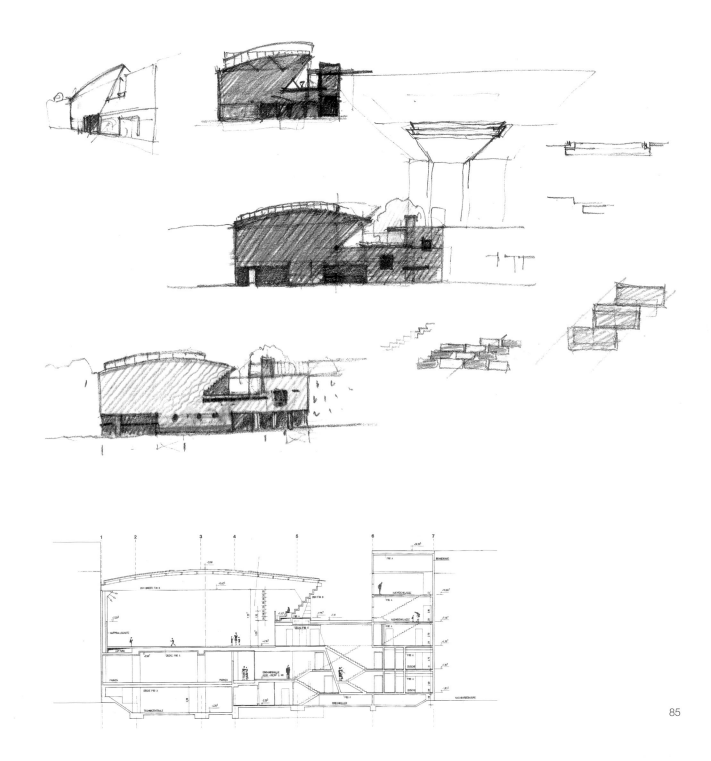

Bebauung Kaiserbadgelände Aachen 1990
Development of the Kaiserbad complex in Aachen 1990

Die Römer hatten hier schon Badehäuser und Lager. Karolus Magnus, in der Region geboren, schien sich auch hier wohl zu fühlen, jedenfalls ließ er gleich nebenan Kapelle und Pfalz errichten. Somit ist der Ort der heißen Quelle auch der Geburtsort der Stadt. Ein großes Badehaus – das Kaiserbad –, im Krieg zerstört, wird ersetzt durch eine kleine Anlage, die wiederum (da unwirtschaftlich), wird ersetzt durch die jetzige Neubebauung, die neben dem Inhalt einiger städtischer Funktionen im Wesentlichen zur Aufgabe hatte, den freien Blick auf den Dom zu belassen und dem Quellort einen angemessenen Rahmen zu geben.

The Romans once had attractive baths and camps here. Charlemagne, who was born in the region, also appears to have felt at home here; at any rate he had the palace chapel (palatinate) built immediately adjacent. As such the location of the hot spring is also the city's birthplace. A large baths house – known as the Kaiserbad or Emperor's Bath, was destroyed during World War II and was replaced by a smaller one. As the latter proved unviable it was replaced by the current new development. Apart from housing a number of municipal facilities, its main task was to provide an unimpeded view of the cathedral and create an appropriate setting for the spa.

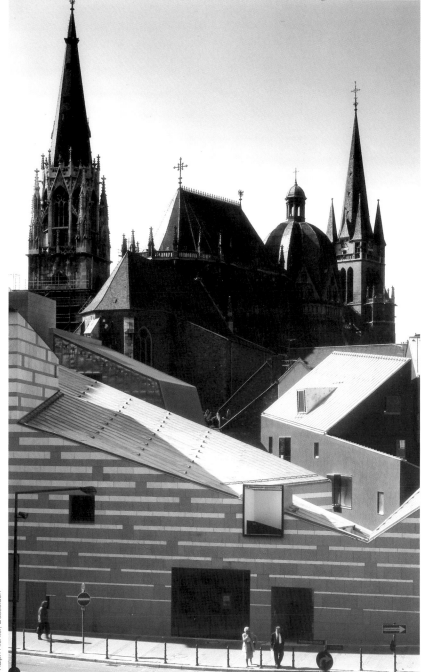

© Ralph Richter, Düsseldorf

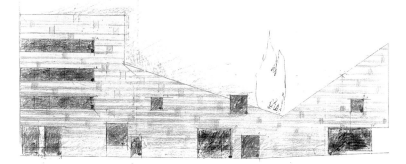

Bebauung Kaiserbadgelände Aachen 1990
Development of the Kaiserbad complex in Aachen 1990

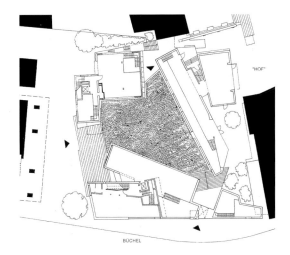

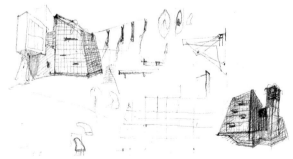

Bebauung Kaiserbadgelände Aachen 1990
Development of the Kaiserbad complex in Aachen 1990

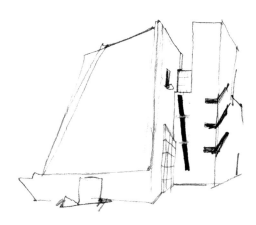

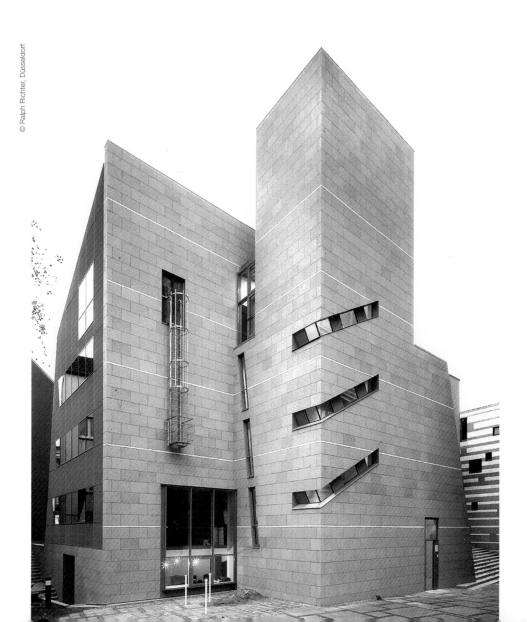

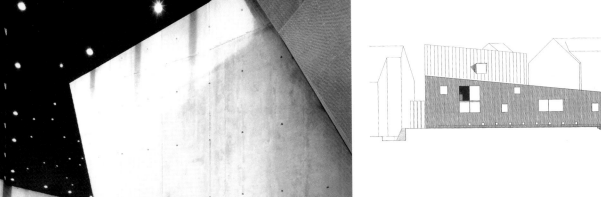

Bebauung Kaiserbadgelände Aachen 1990
Development of the Kaiserbad complex in Aachen 1990

Synagoge Aachen 1991
Synagogue in Aachen 1991

An dem Ort, an dem von „braunen Horden" in der Kristallnacht die damalige Synagoge niedergebrannt wurde, ein neues Stück Stadt dachten wir, eine Synagoge (Tempel), ein Versammlungsraum (Platz), ein Garten für das Laubhüttenfest (Park), ein Bad, eine Schule und eine Reihe von Wohnungen, das Programm einer Stadt, ein kleiner städtischer Organismus. Die Synagoge ist als geistiger Ort formuliert, die Ordnung der anderen Bereiche als sinnliches Prinzip, das frei auf den städtischen Kontext reagiert.

The idea was to create a new area of city at the spot where the "Brown Hordes", that is to say the Nazis, burned down the existing synagogue during the Night of the Crystals in November 1938. This small urban organism comprises a synagogue (temple), a place of assembly (square), a garden for the Feast of Tabernacles (park), a ritual bath, a school and a series of apartments. The synagogue is expressed as a spiritual place, the arrangement of the other areas in line with a principle that appeals to the senses while also responding freely to the urban context.

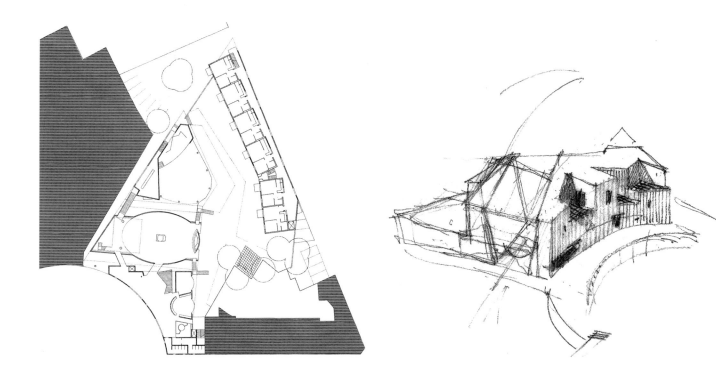

Synagoge Aachen 1991
Synagogue in Aachen 1991

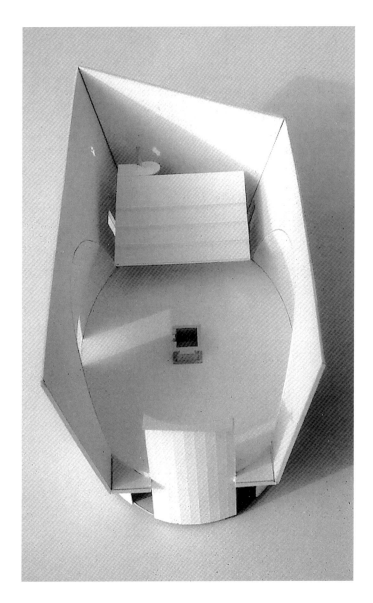

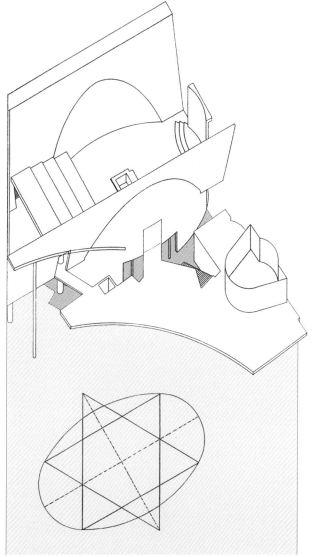

Auffallender als die Vergessenheit des Ortes sind die Maßstabsbrüche zwischen Dorf, Gewerbe und Stadt, die nur erträglich werden durch die weite leere Fläche des Kirmesplatzes. Das Ausbildungshotel Haus Crange kann in dieser Umgebung eine Bedeutung haben, indem es durch Funktion, Form und Volumen zu einer städtebaulichen Ausgewogenheit führt. Die baugeschichtlichen Vorgaben des Hauses, die Einhaltung seiner Grundmauern, die teilweise Verwendung noch vorgefundener Elemente, wie auch die Unversehrtheit seines näheren Umfeldes, geben eine typologisch eindeutige Grundform vor. Der geforderte neue Zugang von Westen und die daraus folgende Bedeutungslosigkeit des ehemaligen östlichen Zugangs führt allerdings zu einem wesentlichen Konflikt. Unser Entwurfsansatz geht von der Lösung dieses Konfliktes aus. Der neue Zugang erschließt die Struktur tangential, ohne die Physiognomie störend zu verändern, und macht damit den Innenhof zum eigentlichen Thema des Entwurfs.

Even more noticeable than the extent to which the location has fallen into neglect is the lack of proportional balance between the village, the industrial estate, and the town, a matter only rendered halfway tolerable by the broad empty space of the fairground. In such a setting, Training Hotel Haus Crange can only make a meaningful statement, if its function, form and volume lead to a greater balance in the overall urban setting. The specifications set by the building's historical fabric (we had to keep to the existing outer line of the walls and in part used existing elements, while also preserving its immediate surroundings intact) also defined the clear basic typological form adopted. The new access required to the West and the subsequent irrelevance of the former East entrance created a real conflict. Our proposal is designed to solve this conflict. The new entrance offer tangential access to the edifice without changing and thus disturbing its physiognomy, highlighting the inner courtyard as the key theme in the new proposal.

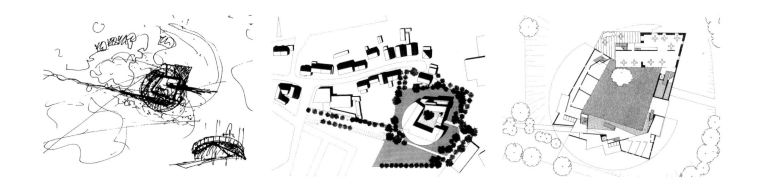

Gesamtschule Viersen 1992
School in Viersen 1992

Es gibt einen 6 m hohen Bahndamm, es gibt eine Gasleitung quer über den Grund, es gibt Wohngebäude, von denen Abstand zu halten ist. In diesem verbleibenden engen Bereich fächert sich dieses Gebäude auf, wie der Flügel einer Glucke, um darunter die Kinder zu schützen.

There is a 6m-high railway embankment and a gas pipe running diagonally across the grounds to be avoided, and the school has to be kept at a distance from the local residential buildings. The building fans outward in the remaining confined space, resembling the wings of a mother hen, with the children sheltering beneath it.

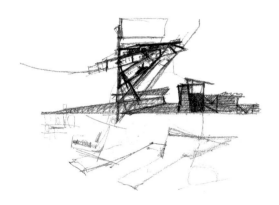

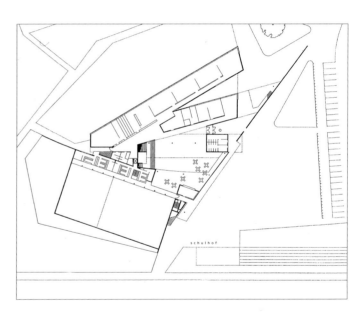

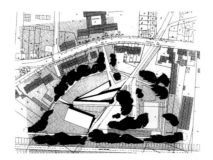

Bebauung „Spitze" Halle 1992
Development "Spitze" in Halle 1992

Dieses Gelände am ehemaligen Ufersumpf der Elbe, „Spitze" genannt, ist entstanden durch Aufschütten mit Asche der Strohfeuer zum Sieden des Salzes. Das Salz hat die Stadt im Mittelalter reich gemacht. In der Hoffnung, ähnliche wirtschaftliche Impulse zu erhalten, sollte das Gelände neu überbaut werden. Institute der nahen Universität, eine Stadthalle, ein Tagungshotel, einige Wohnungen sowie große Verkaufsflächen sollten diesen Grund füllen. Uns war wichtig, das Bild der Flussauen vor der Stadt weitgehend zu erhalten. Daher haben wir das Gelände zur Stadt hin angehoben und die Verkaufsflächen daruntergeschoben, mit einer Gebäudekante zur Stadt hin. Von außen kommend sieht man lediglich ein ansteigendes begrüntes Terrain, in dem vereinzelt Gebäude stehen.

Known as "Spitze", this location on the former marshland lining the Elbe was created by piling up the ashes leftover from straw burnt to boil salt. It was the salt that made the city rich in the Middle Ages. A major motive in redeveloping this zone was to set in motion a similar economic upswing. Institutes for the nearby university, a town hall, a conference hotel, apartments and extensive retail areas are scheduled for the site. A crucial consideration for us was to retain the appearance of the marshland meadows just outside the city as far as possible. This led us to raise the site towards the city, and insert the retail space behind, with one edge of the building facing the city. Approaching from outside you see only a rising green expanse of ground on which buildings are dotted here and there.

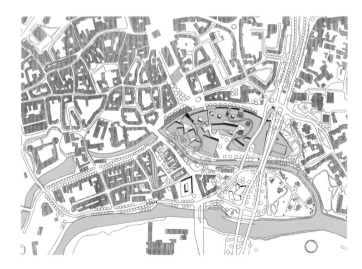
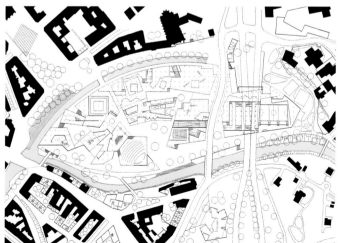

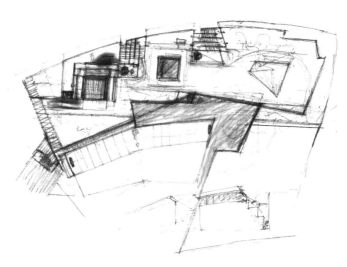

Bebauung „Spitze" Halle 1992
Development "Spitze" in Halle 1992

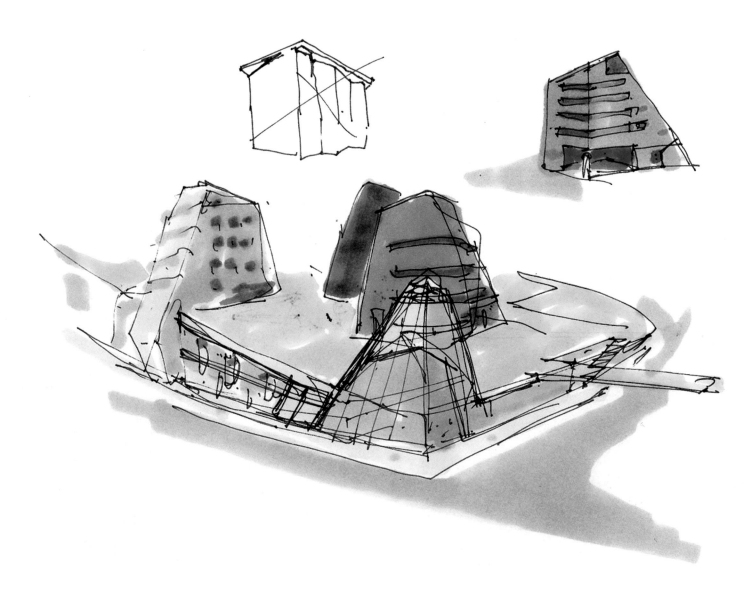

Museum Simeonsstift in Trier 1994
Museum Simeonstift in Trier 1994

Wo wir ergänzen sollten, war einst der Klostergarten mit großen Bäumen. Die Straße und der Busbahnhof haben alles aus dem Gleichgewicht gebracht. Tanzende Türme, von der Dimension alter Bäume, die sich an den Händen fassen, geben dem Vorhandenen seine Würde wieder und dem städtischen Umfeld seine Ausgewogenheit. Die Wunden im Klosterinneren bzw. Museumsinneren sind behutsam mit modernen Mitteln repariert unter Beibehaltung der alten Proportionen. Das Maß ist hier wichtiger als das Material.

The area we were to add to was once the monastery garden with large trees. The road and bus station have completely destroyed the former balance. Dancing towers – the size of old trees – holding each other by the hand restore the dignity to the present environs, and restore the balance in the urban environment. The wounds in the interior of the monastery (now a museum) are carefully repaired using modern means while retaining the former proportions. The scale takes precedence over the materials.

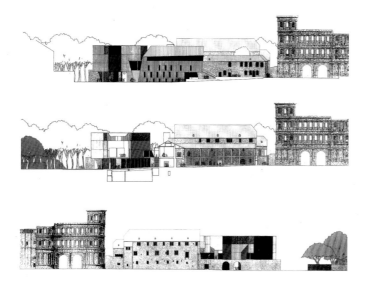
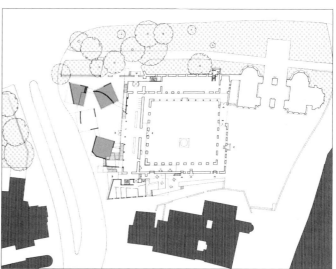

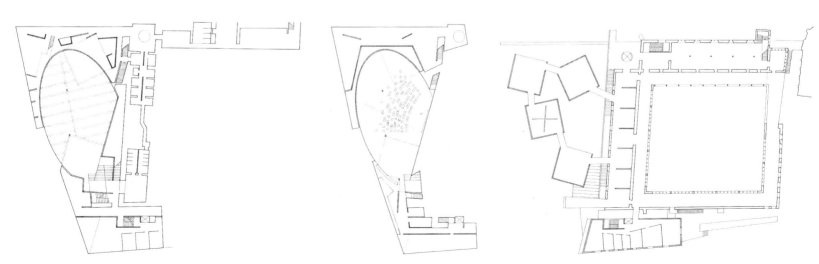

Masterplan Centrum Meerssen 1996 – 2001
Meerssen Master Plan 1996 – 2001

Meerssen, ehemals ein Punkt an einer Landstraße, mit der Zeit eine Addition unterschiedlicher „Biotope", ist zu schade, es mit der „großen Idee" zu zerstören. Stärken wollten wir sie, all die kleinen unterschiedlichen Orte und uns nur den Übergängen widmen. Dem Neuen sollte man ansehen, dass es den gleichen genetischen Code hat. Nur die Wunden sind zu heilen. Manchmal reicht auch ein Baum an der richtigen Stelle, nicht um etwas zu verstecken, sondern um wieder ein Gleichgewicht herzustellen.

Meerssen, once a dot on a country road, with passage of time an addition of different "biotopes", is too precious to be destroyed by imposing a "grand idea" on it. We want to strengthen them, all those small different places, and devote ourselves to the transitions. And the new should reveal the fact that is has the same genetic code. Only the wounds needed to be healed. Sometimes a tree in the right place suffices – not to conceal something, but to restore the right balance.

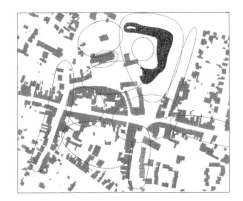 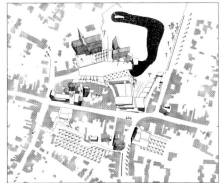 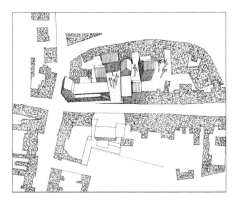

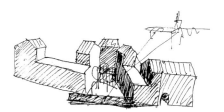

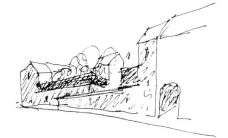

Felix-Nussbaum-Haus Osnabrück 1995
Felix Nussbaum Museum in Osnabrück 1995

Das Haus des Felix Nussbaum
Sträubt sich gegen das Haus,
in dem vielleicht der Name Nussbaum
auf die Liste gesetzt wurde.
Es wird keine Symbiose eingehen,
wird sich nicht mit in die Reihe stellen,
es wird auch kein Haus sein,
es wird nur der Anfang einer Treppe sein,
die nicht weiterführen durfte.

The house of Felix Nussbaum
Objects strongly to the house,
In which perhaps the name Nussbaum
Was put on a list.
It will not enter into symbiosis,
Will refuse to close ranks with others,
It will also not be a house,
It will only be the beginning of a staircase,
That was not able to go further.

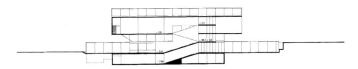

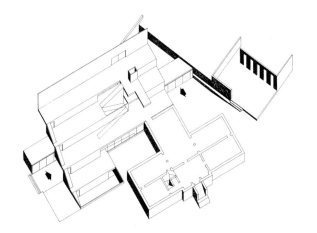

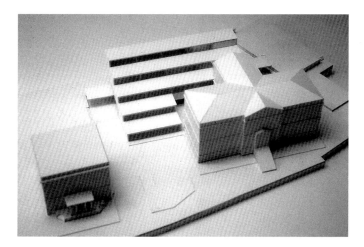

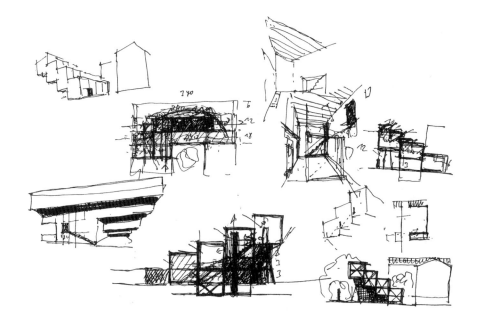

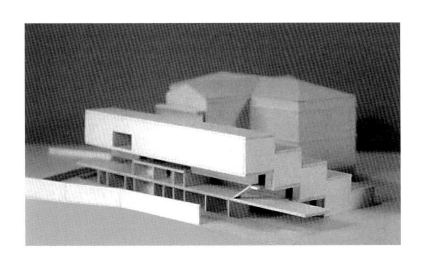

Internationales Handelszentrum Düsseldorf „Fenster zum Park" Düsseldorf 1995
Window looking onto park in Düsseldorf 1995

Ein großes Fenster stemmt sich dem riesigen Park entgegen. Zu seinen Füßen ein schmaler Platz, Restaurants und Geschäfte. Ein Kindergarten und 72 Wohnungen füllen das Gemäuer.

A huge window asserts itself against an enormous park. At its feet stand a narrow square, restaurants and stores. The walls are filled by a kindergarten and 72 apartments.

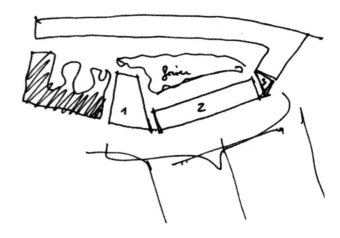

Archäologisches Museum Herne 1997
Archaeology Museum in Herne 1997

Das Ehemalige ist durch Krieg und Nachkrieg im Wesentlichen zerstört. Die Reanimation des Vergangenen, mit Museumsfunktionen besetzte Häuser, sind Schatten und Dach der tiefliegenden Ausstellungsebene. Die „Häuser", zu Hohlkörpern geformt, haben eine weittragende Funktion. Die Spuren des Alten geben so dem Neuen die Form. Das alles überdeckende Glasdach ist mit Siliziumelementen so bestückt, dass, wo gewünscht, Licht bis in die untersten Ebenen fällt.

The former museum was largely destroyed during World War II and in the years thereafter. In this reanimation of the past, those buildings housing various museum facilities provide both shade and roofing for the lower-lying exhibition level. The "shells" extend out over the lower level. As a consequence, the remains of the old define the design of the new. Silicon elements are so arranged in the glazed roof covering the entire ensemble that light can penetrate through into the lowest storeys where desired.

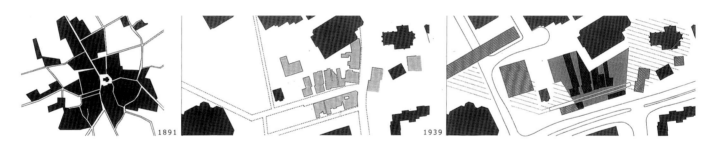

1891   1939

wer seine spuren vernichtet, vernichtet auch seine geschichte

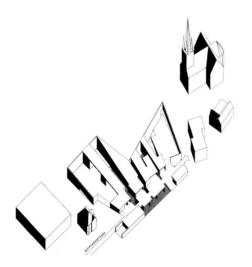

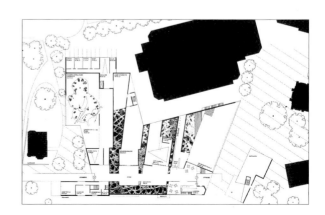

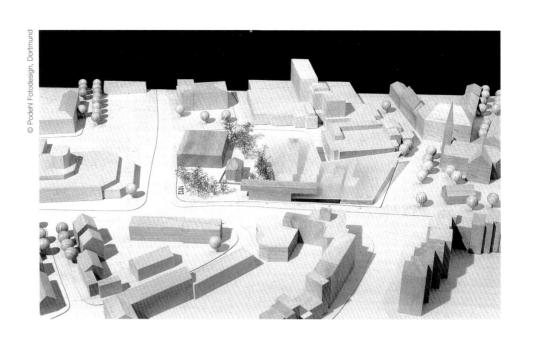

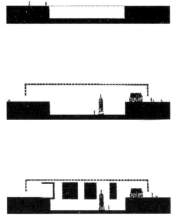

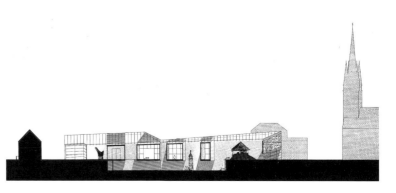

Maria-Montessor-Gesamtschule „Am Moltkebahnhof" 1998 – 2001
Maria Montessori School in Aachen 1998 – 2001

Wenn der Ort mit der neuen Schule eine andere Bedeutung bekommt, muss auch der Schule an diesem Ort eine andere Bedeutung als üblich zukommen. Ein Viertel der arbeitsfähigen Bevölkerung wird auf lange Sicht ohne Arbeit sein, ohne das, was wir bisher als Arbeit verstehen. Unser Leben wird sich anders organisieren müssen. In Italien gibt es seit längerem das Modell des lebenslangen Lernens und Lehrens. Das heißt, jeder ist zeitweise Schüler und Lehrer, manchmal ein paar Stunden, ein oder zwei halbe Wochentage, manchmal über längere Zeit. Lernen und Lehren ist nicht mehr Frage des Lebensabschnittes. „Die erziehende Stadt." Ort der Vermittlung zwischen den Generationen. Das Netz der territorialen Bildungsagenturen stellt den bevorzugten Entwicklungsraum für neue Erziehungsverhältnisse zwischen den Generationen dar. Seine Verortung außerhalb des Schulsystems ermöglicht innerhalb des einzelnen Projekts / der einzelnen Einrichtung die Einbindung brach-liegender, freiwilliger Bildungskräfte (Eltern, Großeltern, Singles), die normalerweise im professionellen Rahmen schulischer Bildungsarbeit nicht zugelassen sind. Eine strukturelle Verbindung mit dem Schulsystem garantiert in jedem Fall die gleichwertige Anerkennung der in ihm gemachten Bildungserfahrungen. Damit bildet das Netz territorialer Bildungsagenturen die angemessene Umgebung für ein neues Selbstverständnis „lebensbegleitenden Lernens", ergänzt durch die soziale Aufgabe eines „lebensbegleitenden Lehrens": bürgerschaftliche Bildungssolidarität aller Generationen. (Quelle: Luigi Guerra „Die Erziehende Stadt")

If the area gains a new significance through the construction of a new school, then the latter must also be given a meaning unlike the usual one if located here. A quarter of the population able to pursue gainful employment will be without work in the long run, will be without what we have hitherto understood work to be. Our life will have to be organized differently. In Italy for some time now there has been a model for life-long learning and teaching. In other words, everyone is both student and teacher at some point, some-times for a few hours, sometimes for one or two half-days during the week, sometimes for far longer. Learning and teaching is no longer a matter of a specific time in life. "The educating town". The place where generations meet. The network of territorial edu-cational agencies constitutes the preferred space in which to develop the new educational and inter-generational relationship. By locating it outside the school system, each individual project / individual institution can be linked to voluntary educational capacity that has laid fallow (parents, grandparents, singles) who normally are not allocated a role in the professionally framework of edu-cational work in schools. At any rate, a structural connection to the school system guarantees equal due recognition of the educational experience made in it. In other words, the network of territorial educational agencies forms the appropriate setting for a new self-understanding "life-accompanying learning", supplemented by the social task of "life-accompanying teaching": civil educational solidarity across all the generations. (Source: Luigi Guerra "Die Erziehende Stadt")

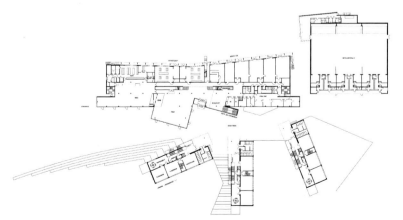

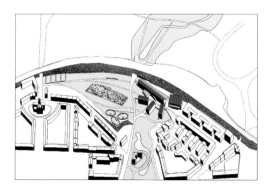

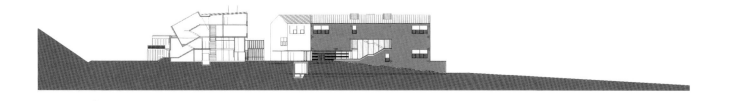

Maria Montessori Gesamtschule „Am Moltkebahnhof" 1998 – 2001
Maria Montessori School in Aachen 1998 – 2001

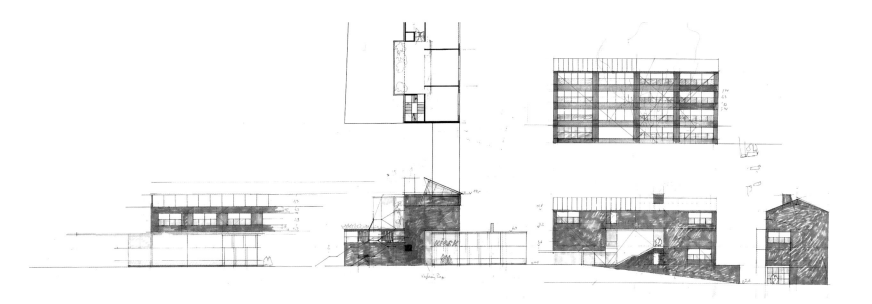

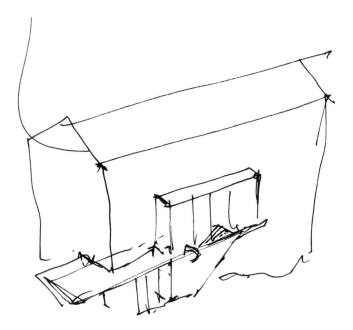

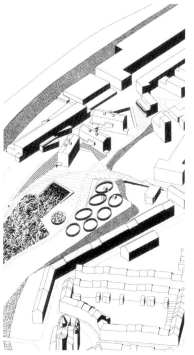

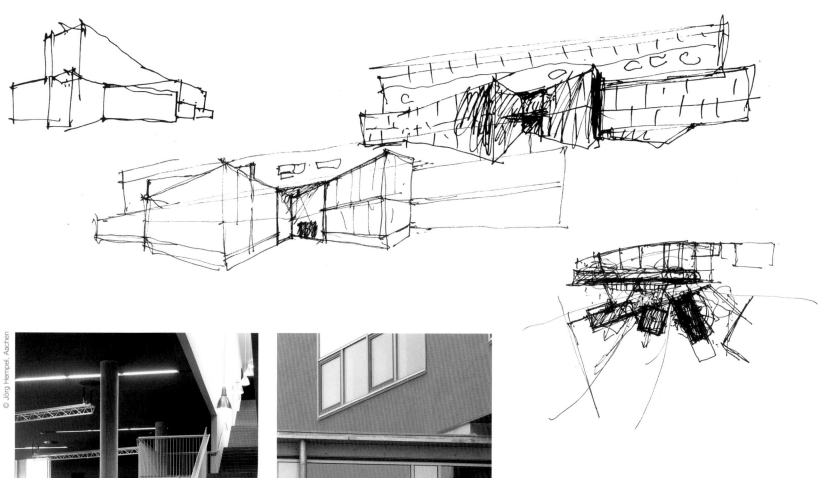

Kulturzentrum Paderborn 2000
Cultural Center in Paderborn 2000

Die Mauern in dieser Stadt, der helle Kalkstein, die hohen Wände, die Klarheit der Baukörper, das Wasser in allen Farben und Bewegungen, der Klang des Wassers, der Klang der Farben, der Klang der Gebäude miteinander, das Ganze als ein Stück Stadt, ein Teil Paderborns, das ist es, was wir umsetzen wollten. Und jedes Haus liegt am Wasser, hat seine Terrassen, hat steinerne Gärten im Wasser, Gärten, in denen aufgrund des umfliessenden Wassers der Boden nie friert, Seerosengärten. Und ein langer Steg über das Wasser führt zur Stadt hinaus.

The walls in this city, the bright limestone, the high façades, the clarity of the edifices, the countless colors and movements of the water, the sound of the water, the sound of the water, the sound of the colors, the sound of the buildings together, the entirety as a part of the city, a part of Paderborn – that is what we wanted to achieve. And each house stood by the water, had patios, had stone gardens in the water, gardens in which owing to the water flowing around them, the ground never freezes, lily gardens. And a long jetty over the water leads out to the city.

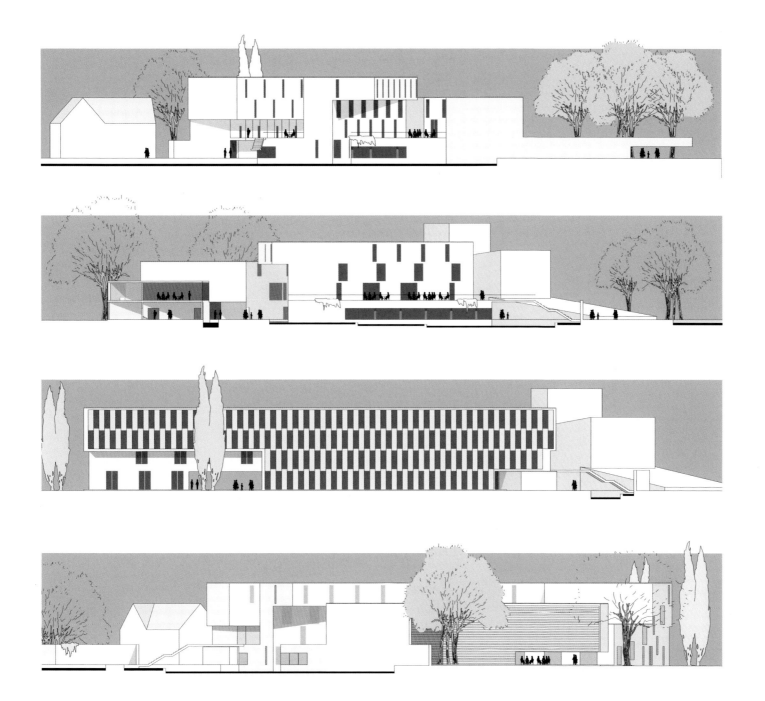

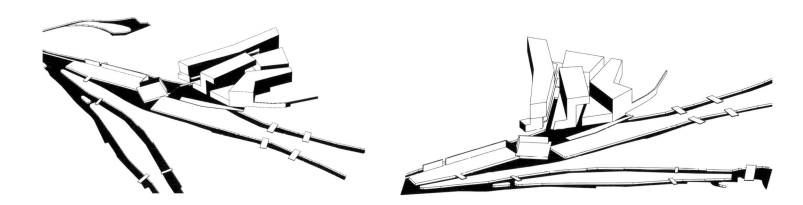

Rathaus Bernried 2002
Town Hall and Community Center in Bernried 2002

Es gibt zwei geschlossene Bauformen in Bernried, das Kloster und den großen Hof am See, die dritte Großform – das Rathaus mit dem Gemeindezentrum – sollte eine offene sein. Neben dem Kloster mit dem Klosterhof ist das Rathaus mit dem Dorfplatz der zweite Pol des Ortes. Der Höhenunterschied von zehn Metern zwischen dem neuen Dorfplatz und dem Grund über dem Sommerkeller erwies sich als das eigentliche Problem. Das Rathaus steht im Kernort, ist aber auch Teil der umliegenden Ortsteile. Wir haben versucht, beidem gerecht zu werden, ein Rathaus zu planen, das einerseits am Dorfplatz steht, andererseits auf der Höhe oberhalb des Sommerkellers allen dient, indem wir dort mit dem Gemeindezentrum einen zweiten Platz, den Rathausplatz, vorsehen, mit einem herrlichen Blick auf und über den See. Somit liegt also die Legislative mit Ratssaal und Bürgermeisteramt zum Dorfplatz, die Exekutive, die reine Verwaltung eben, zum Rathausplatz mit dem Gemeindezentrum.

There are two closed structures in Bernried, the monastery and the large courtyard by the lake. The plan was for the third large edifice – the Town Hall with the Community Center – to be an open structure. Alongside the monastery and the Klosterhof (monastery courtyard) the Town Hall on the village square is the second focal point in Bernried. The central problem proved to be the ten meters difference in altitude between the new village square and the ground covering the Sommerkeller (summer cellars). Though the Town Hall stands in the heart of the town it also serves the surrounding districts. We tried to do justice to both these concepts; to design a Town Hall that stands on the village square, yet incorporating the elevation above the Sommerkeller by locating the Community Center on a second square (originally to be the Rathausplatz), with a magnificent view onto and out across the lake. Consequently, the legislative (comprising the Council Chambers and mayor's office) face the village square, while the executive, in other words the administration faces onto Rathausplatz with the Community Center.

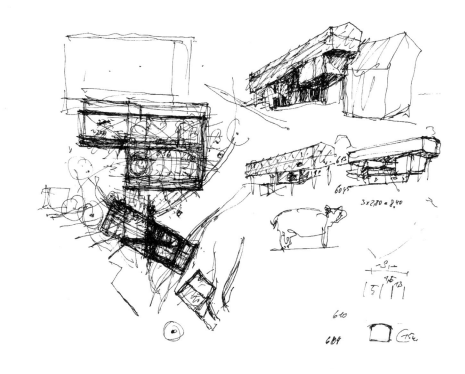

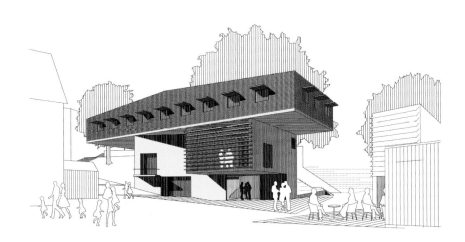

Rathaus und Wohnbebauung Winseler / L 2002
Town Hall and Residential Development Center in Winseler / L 2002

Oben an der kleinen Kirche ist Raum, unten, wo das Rathaus stehen soll, nur Wiese. Man muss auf oben reagieren, diagonal versetzt. Die neuen Häuser sind so mächtig wie die vorhandenen. Oben stehen sie in der Reihe, die neuen unten versammeln sich wie freie Bürger um ihr Rathaus.

Higher up, near the small church, there is open space, below where the Town Hall will stand, there are only meadows. You need to respond to the situation above and position the Town Hall set diagonally to one side in terms of the axis of the church. The new buildings are as massive as those already standing. While the new houses above are arranged in rows, those below congregrate around their Town Hall like free citizens.

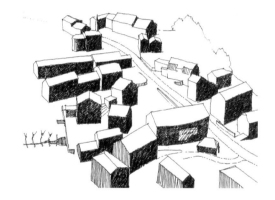

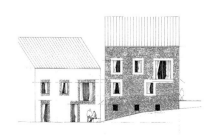

Wir haben das Thema andersherum betrachtet. Wir stehen innerhalb der Mauer, sehen die Mauer nicht als Prinzip des Wegsperrens, sondern als Prinzip des Aussperrens an, begeben uns in den Schutz der Mauer. Wir betreten eine andere Welt, gehen in Klausur, was wir als Chance ansehen. Wir entwickeln ein Konzept, in dem die Welt bewusst nach innen gekehrt ist, in dem der Blick auf die Mauern möglichst vermieden wird. Alle Fassaden gehen nach innen! Als architektonische Ansätze dienen uns Beispiele aus Zeiten und Kulturen, in denen sich das Leben autonom innerhalb von Mauern abspielte. Der Park wird von dreigeschossigen Zellentrakten umringt. Das Band der Zellen ist jeweils als Drittelkreis in einen rechten Winkel eingelegt. Die Zonierung innerhalb der Verkehrsflächen ist so günstiger, das Licht fällt weicher auf die gekrümmte Wand, harte Konturen sind vermieden. Der Park ist das Herz der Anlage. Die gebogenen Flächen der Zellen stellen sich als autonome großmaßstäbliche Gitterstruktur dar. Unterschiedlich farbige Lüftungsflügel innerhalb der Großstruktur sorgen für eine gewisse Individualität.

We approached the topic the other way round. We stand inside the walls and do not see the walls as a principle of being locked away but as the principles of locking things out, and thus place ourselves within the protection of the walls. We enter a different world, opt for a retreat, construe this as an opportunity. We develop a concept in which the world is deliberately turned inward, in which wherever possible any view of the walls is avoided. All the façades are aimed inwards! As architectural models, we chose examples from ages and cultures in which life took place independently within walls. The park is surrounded by a three-storey building containing the cells. The ribbon of cells is designed respectively as a third of a circle inserted into a right angle. This renders zoning within the transport areas easier, light falls more softly on the curved wall, and we avoided harsh contours. The park forms the heart of the plant. The curved surfaces of the cells function as an autonomous grid structure with large proportions. Differently colored ventilation wings within the main structure create a sense of individuality.

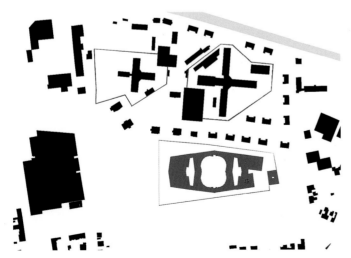

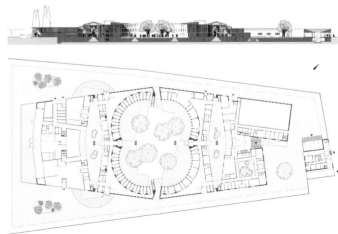

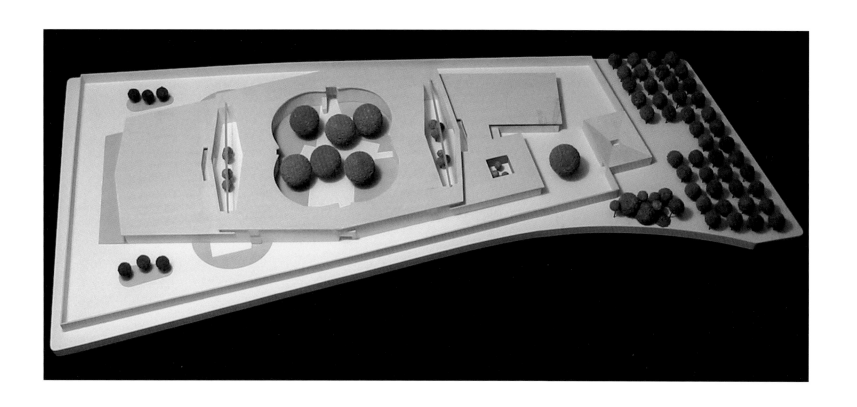

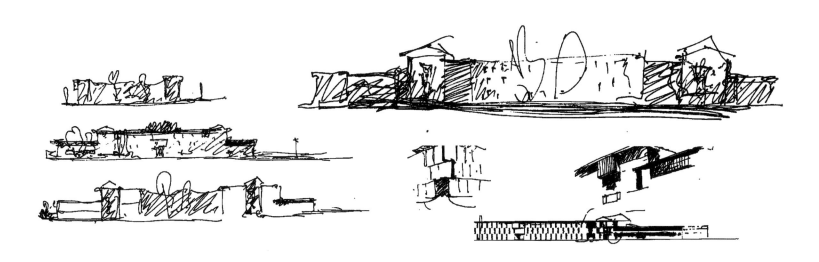

Akademie-Galerie Düsseldorf 2005
Akademie-Galerie in Düsseldorf 2005

Dem Wunsch der Düsseldorfer Kunstakademie, einen angemessenen Ort für ihre Sammlung zu finden (darunter auch eine Zeichnung von Raffael), vor allem aber auch einen angemessenen Ort für die Werke und Nachlässe ihrer ehemaligen, jetzigen und zukünftigen Lehrer, kommt die Stadt Düsseldorf entgegen durch das Angebot, das Erdgeschoss der ehemaligen Kunstgewerbeschule am Burgplatz zur Verfügung zu stellen, an einem Ort, der als ehemaliger Seitenflügel des Schlosses die so genannte Malerschule beherbergte, die einst den Flammen zum Opfer fiel.

The City of Düsseldorf has responded to the wish of the Düsseldorf Kunstakademie to find a suitable location for its collection (which includes a drawing by Raphael), but above all an appropriate place for the works and estates of its former, present and future professors. The City has made available the ground floor of the former Arts & Crafts College at Burgplatz; years ago this was the wing of the castle and housed the so-called Malerschule, which was destroyed by fire.

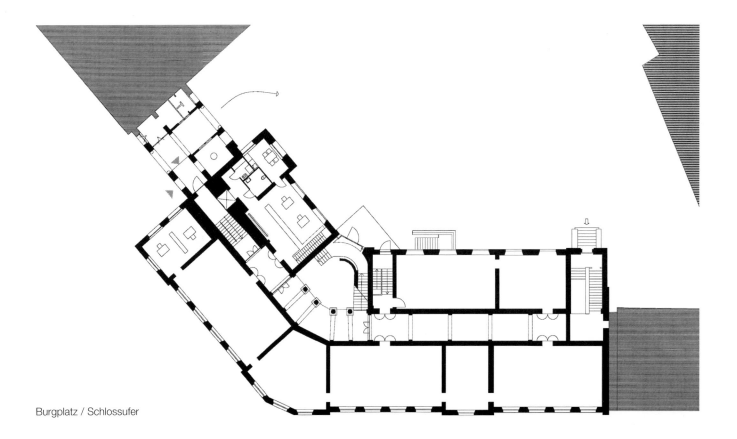

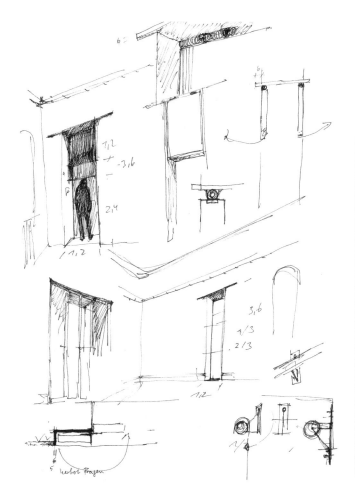

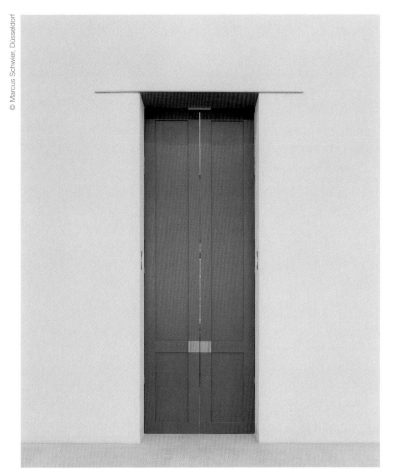

Stubengasse Münster 2004
Development "Stubengasse" in Münster 2004

Zwei große Volumen, die städtischen Raum formulieren sollen, waren Vorgabe und Ausgangspunkt. Wir haben jedoch die Kanten härter gefasst, um sinnliche Raumqualitäten zu erhalten. Die beiden Groß-volumen sind als Dimension erhalten, da wir überzeugt waren, Maß-stäblichkeit nur über sinnvolle Strukturierung, nicht über vorgetäuschte Parzellierung zu erreichen. Wir haben uns zwei große freundliche schlafende Tiere vorgestellt, die mit ihrer Umgebung eine Familie bilden, aber trotzdem autonom sind. Die Strukturen sind fließend wie ein Fell, nicht additiv. Nichts ist zufällig, es gibt Regeln, die dem genetischen Code der Stadt entnommen sind. Änderungen sind innerhalb der Regeln unproblematisch, die Variationsbreite ist sehr groß. Das leuchtende Ziegelrot dieser Stadt wollen wir, aber geschichtet zwischen hellem Grau, von der Wirkung eines Hologramms. Das Grau mit eingestreutem dunklen Ziegel bildet den Fond für die präzise gesetzten roten Linien.

Our brief and the starting point: two large volumes designed such as to lend expression to the urban setting. However, we formulated the outlines more distinctly in order to maintain sensual spatial qualities. We opted to retain the dimensions of the two large volumes, since we were convinced that the desired sense of scale could only be achieved using logical structuring and not through simulated division into smaller plots. We imagined two large, friendly, sleeping animals that form a family with their surroundings, and yet remain autonomous. The structures flow like the lines of a pelt rather than a patchwork composition. Nothing is arbitrary; instead there are rules derived from the town's genetic code. Alterations can be made while yet observing these rules and the scope for variations is huge. What we want is the town's bright brick red, but sandwiched between pale gray so the effect is like that of a hologram. The gray with its spattering of dark tiles forms the backdrop against which the precisely placed red lines stand out.

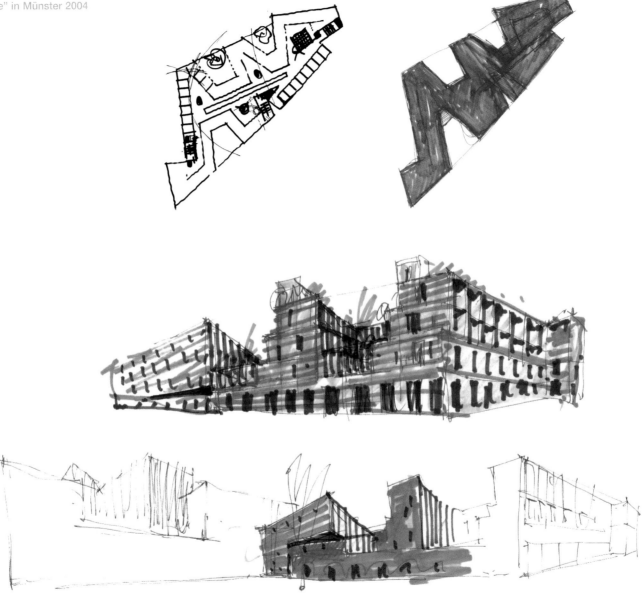

Ernst Kasper

1935	Geboren in Trier. Vater Bergmann Linksrheinisches Kohlenrevier
1939 – 56	Abitur am Humanistischen Gymnasium in Geldern Arbeit im Bergbau Praktikum als Maurer
1956 – 63	Studium an der RWTH Aachen. Studentische Mitarbeit am Lehrstuhl Prof. Mertens
1963	Diplomarbeit. Auszeichnung: Förderpreis Bundesverband der Deutschen Industrie
1963 – 64	Wissenschaftlicher Assistent am Schulbauinstitut Prof. Fritz Eller, RWTH Aachen
Ab 1964	Eigenes Architekturbüro in Aachen
Bis 1965	In Partnerschaft mit Karl Wimmenauer
	Programme für Schulzentren und Gesamtschulen Zahlreiche prämierte Schulbau-Wettbewerbe
1971	Ruf an die Kunstakademie Düsseldorf als Professor für Baukunst
Ab 1972	Als „Planungsgruppe Kasper" Partnerschaften mit:
1972 – 2002	Prof. Klaus Klever
1972 – 77	Dipl. Ing. Heinrich Dahmen
1977 – 80	Dipl. Ing. Mechthild Kaiser
2000	Emeritus
Seit 1999	Gastprofessur an der Scuola Arquitectura der Universidad Austral in Chile

Ernst Kasper

1935	Born in Trier. Father miner in the coal-mining area Linksrheinisches Kohlenrevier
1939 – 56	A levels at classics grammar school Works as miner Apprenticeship as bricklayer
1956 – 63	Studies at the Technical University of Aachen (RWTH). Assists Prof. Mertens
1963	Dissertation. Distinction: award from the Federal Association of German Industry (BDI)
1963 – 64	Academic assistant at School Design Institute Prof. Fritz Eller, RWTH Aachen
As of 1964	Own architect's office in Aachen
until 1965	with Karl Wimmenauer as partner
	Projects for school centers and comprehensive schools Wins numerous awards in school design competitions
1971	Appointment to Kunstakademie Düsseldorf as Professor of Architecture
As of 1972	Planungsgruppe Kasper (Kasper Planning Group) Partners with:
1972 – 2002	Prof. Klaus Klever
1972 – 77	qualified engineer Heinrich Dahmen
1977 – 80	qualified engineer Mechthild Kaiser
2000	Emeritus
As of 1999	Visiting professorship at the Scuola Arquitectura der Universidad Austral in Chile

Alle Projekte all Projects 1972 – 2003 als as „Planungsgruppe Kasper": mit with Heinrich Dahmen bis until 1977 / mit with Klaus Klever bis until 2003 / mit with Mechthild Kaiser 1978 – 1980

1964
Realschule Intermediate
School **Blankenheim**
Wettbewerb 4. Preis
Competition 4th Prize
AG mit in collaboration with
Harald Schmuck

1965
Volksschule Elementary
School **Nideggen**
Wettbewerb 1. Preis
Competition 1st Prize

1965
Realschule Secondary
School **Wegberg**
Wettbewerb 1. Preis
Competition 1st Prize
AG mit in collaboration with
Karl Wimmenauer
Realisiert Realized 1969
Auftraggeber Client
Stadt City of **Wegberg**

1966
Jugendzentrum Youth
Center **Unna-Fröndenberg**
Wettbewerb 2. Preis
Competition 2nd Prize
AG mit in collaboration with
Karl Wimmenauer und and
Georg Ismer

1966
Krankenhaus
Hospital **Lage**
Wettbewerb Competition
AG mit in collaboration with
Richard Plückebaum

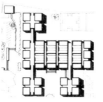

1966
Gewerbliche Schulen
Vocational Colleges **Düren**
Wettbewerb Competition
Ankauf Purchased design
AG mit in collaboration with
Karl Wimmenauer

1967
Wohnviertel Residential
District **Bochum**
Wettbewerb Competition
AG mit in collaboration with
Karl Wimmenauer

1968
Schulzentrum Sek. I
Lower Secondary School
Center **Bergisch Gladbach**
Paffrath
Wettbewerb Competition
Ankauf Purchased design

1968
Revierpark Mining Park
Nienhausen
Wettbewerb Competition

1969
Grund- und Sonderschule
Primary and Special School
Köln-Flittard
Wettbewerb 2. Preis
Competition 2nd Prize

1969
Grundschule
Primary School
Meerbusch-Büderich
Wettbewerb 1. Preis
Competition 1st Prize
AG mit in collaboration with
Heinrich Speckhan
Realisiert Realized 1972
Auftraggeber Client
Stadt City of **Meerbusch**

1969
Hauptschule Secondary
General School **Simmerath**
Wettbewerb 1. Preis
Competition 1st Prize

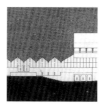

1969
Schulzentrum Sek. I Lower
Secondary School Center
Bergisch Gladbach
Ahornweg

1970
Grundschule Primary
School **Hennef-Sieg**
Wettbewerb 2. Preis
Competition 2nd Prize

1970
Grundschule Primary
School **Neuss-Erfttal**
Wettbewerb 2. Preis
Competition 2nd Prize
AG mit in collaboration with
Heinrich Speckhan

1970
Hauptschule
Secondary General School
Geilenkirchen
Wettbewerb 4. Preis
Competition 4th Prize

1970
Gewerbliche Schulen
Vocational Colleges **Aachen**
Wettbewerb Competition
Ankauf Purchased design

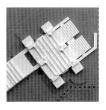

1970
Gesamtschule Sek. I Lower
Secondary Modern School
Nürnberg-Langwasser
Wettbewerb Competition
AG mit in collaboration with
SLS Planungsgruppe

1970
Schulzentrum Sek. I
Lower Secondary School
Center **Blankenheim**
Raumprogramm und
Vorentwurf 1. Fassung
Room program and
predesign 1st version

1971
Real- und Sonderschule
Intermediate and Special
School **Köln-Müngersdorf**
Wettbewerb

1971
Haus Funke Funke
Residence / **Entwurf 1-4 /**
1971-1981
Beauftragt Commissioned
Auftraggeber Client:
Ehepaar Funke
Nicht realisiert not realized

1971
Schulzentrum Sek. I Lower
Secondary School Center
Horrem
Wettbewerb 1. Preis
Competition 1st Prize

1971
Schulzentrum Sek. I Lower
Secondary School Center
Meerbusch
Wettbewerb 2. Preis
Competition 2nd Prize
AG mit in collaboration with
Heinrich Speckhan

1973
Verwaltungsgebäude
City Admin. Building
Herzogenrath
Wettbewerb Competition

1973
Seehotel Freilingen
Seehotel Freilingen
Gutachten Expert opinion

1973
Revierpark Mining Park
Mattlerbusch
Gutachten Expert opinion
AG mit in collaboration with
Peter Latz

1973
Grundschule Primary
School **Brühl-West**
Beauftragung
Commissioned
AG mit in collaboration with
Rudolf Sandhoff
Realisiert Realized 1973
Auftraggeber Client:
Stadt Brühl

1974
Heizwerk und Müllverbren-
nungsanlage Heating and
Waste Incineration Unit **der**
for **RWTH Aachen**
Beauftragung
Commissioned
AG mit in collaboration with
Heinrich Speckhan
Realisiert Realized 1976
Auftraggeber Client: **Land**
NRW State of North Rhine
Westphalia **vertreten durch**
represented by **Staats-**
hochbauamt State Building
Office **der** of **RWTH Aachen**
Generalplanung General
planning: **STEAG Essen**

1975
Gymnasium High School
Viersen „Auf der Loeh"
Wettbewerb Competition

1975
Grundschule Primary
School **Ahlen**
Wettbewerb Competition
Ankauf Purchased design

1975
Grundschule Primary
School **Erftstadt Lechenich**
Wettbewerb Competition

1975
Berufsschulen Vocational
colleges **in Kempen und**
and **Viersen – Dülken**
Wettbewerb 1. Preis
Competition 1st Prize
AG mit in collaboration with
Heinz Döhmen
Realisiert Realized 1977
Auftraggeber Client:
Kreis Viersen Viersen
District Council

1976
Schulzentrum School
Center Korschenbroich
Wettbewerb 3. Preis
Competition 3rd Prize
AG mit in collaboration with
Heinz Döhmen

1976
Berufsschulzentrum in
Köln-Hürth
Wettbewerb Competition
Ankauf Purchased design

1976
Sanierungskonzept
Innenstadt Concept for
restoring downtown Viersen
Gutachten Expert opinion
AG mit in collaboration with
Heinz Döhmen

1976
Kunstsammlung Art
Collection Düsseldorf
Wettbewerb Competition

1976
Bürgerzentrum Civil Center
Bad Neuenahr-Ahrweiler
Wettbewerb Competition

1977
Kurmittelzentrum Spa
Center Burtscheid
Wettbewerb Competition
AG mit Heinz Döhmen
in collaboration with

1977
Fortbildungseinrichtung
der Justizbehörde Advance
Training Center for the
Judiciary Recklinghausen
Wettbewerb Competition

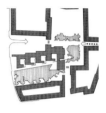

1977
Rathauserweiterung
Extension to Town Hall
Hattingen
Wettbewerb 1. Preis
Competition 1st Prize

1978
Sanierung Restoration of
Schnellengasse
Eschweiler
Wettbewerb Competition

1978
Stiftisch-Humanistisches
Gymnasium Stiftisch-
Humanistic High School
Mönchengladbach
Wettbewerb 1. Preis
Competition 1st Prize
AG mit in collaboration with
Heinz Döhmen
Realisiert Realized 1984
Auftraggeber Client:
Stadt City of
Mönchengladbach

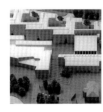

1978
Rathaus und
Stadtbibliothek Town Hall
and Municipal Library
Viersen
Wettbewerb 1. Preis
Competition 1st Prize
AG mit in collaboration with
Heinz Döhmen

1978
Kreishaus und Forum
District Hall and Forum in
Viersen
Wettbewerb 1. Preis
Competition 1st Prize
AG mit in collaboration with
Heinz Döhmen
Realisiert Realized 1984
Auftraggeber Client:
Kreis Viersen Viersen
District Council
Genehmigungsplanung
und „Künstlerische
Oberleitung" Approvals
planning and "Artistic
Supervision"
Generalplanung durch
General planning by
IGR m.b.H, Ratingen

1979
Museum Ludwig Museum
Ludwig Aachen
Wettbewerb 5. Preis
Competition 5th Prize

1980
Rathaus Town Hall
Dortmund
Wettbewerb 2. Preis
Competition 2nd Prize

1980
Justizbehörden Courts
Building Dortmund
Wettbewerb 1. Preis
Competition 1st Prize
AG mit in collaboration with
Heinz Döhmen
Auftraggeber Client:
Land NRW State of North
Rhine Westphalia vertreten
durch represented by
Staatshochbauamt State
Building Office Dortmund
Genehmigungsplanung
Approvals planning
Nicht realisiert Not realized

1980
Postamt Post Office
Dortmund
Gutachten Expert opinion

 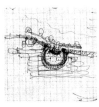     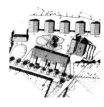

1980
Museum Witten
Gutachten Expert opinion
1. Rang Ranked 1

1982
Landesmuseum für
Technik und Arbeit
Mannheim
Wettbewerb Competition

1983
Germanisches
Nationalmuseum Nürnberg
Nuremberg
Wettbewerb Competition
Künstlerische Beratung
Artistic consultant
Erwin Heerich, Walter
Hofmann

1983
Abfallverwertungsanlage
Waste Recycling Plant **der**
Stadt City of **Frankfurt**
Wettbewerb Competition

1983
Kulturzentrum Cultural
Center **Bergkamen**
Wettbewerb Competition

1983
Ortsmitte Inner Town Zone
Meerbusch
Wettbewerb Competition
AG mit in collaboration with
Heinz Döhmen

1985
Stadtbibliothek und
Museum Municipal Library
and Museum **Münster**
Wettbewerb Competition
1. Fassung 1st Version
1. Preis 1st Prize

1985
Fortbildungseinrichtung
der Finanzverwaltung
NRW mit Internat
Advanced Training Center
for the North Rhine
Westphalia Fiscal Authorities
with Boarding School
in Münster
Wettbewerb Competition

1985
Sparkasse am Ostwall in
Krefeld
Wettbewerb 3. Preis
Competition 3rd Prize
AG mit in collaboration with
Heinz Döhmen

1985
Oberpostdirektion Köln
Cologne Upper Post Office
Gutachten 2. Preis
Directorate 2nd Prize
AG mit in collaboration with
Heinz Döhmen

1985
Kunstpalast Art Palace
Düsseldorf
Wettbewerb Competition
Künstlerische Beratung
Artistic Consultant
Erwin Heerich

1985
Rathaus und Pfarrzentrum
Town Hall and Vicarage
Wittlich
Wettbewerb 2. Preis
Competition 2nd Prize

1986
Goethe-Institut München
Munich
Wettbewerb 3. Preis
Competition 3rd Prize

1986
Klostergarten Abtei Kamp
Monastery Garden, Kamp
Abbey
Wettbewerb Competition
AG mit in collaboration with
Jan Pieper

1986
Thermalbad Thermal Baths
Aachen
Gutachten Expert opinion

1986
„Kleines Haus" "Small
House" **in Braunschweig**
Wettbewerb Competition

Alle Projekte all Projects 1972 – 2003 als as „Planungsgruppe Kasper": mit with Heinrich Dahmen bis until 1977 / mit with Klaus Klever bis until 2003 / mit with Mechthild Kaiser 1978 – 1980

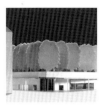      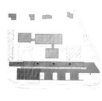 

1986
Marienplatz in München
Munich
Wettbewerb Competition
AG mit in collaboration with
Jutta Cieslock

1986
Berufsbildende Schulen
Vocational Colleges in
Eschweiler
Wettbewerb Competition

1987
Bibliothek und
Stadtmuseum Library and
Municipal Museum am
Hexenturm in Jülich
Wettbewerb 1. Preis
Competition 1ˢᵗ Prize
AG mit in collaboration with
Heinz Döhmen
Realisiert Realized 1991
Auftraggeber Client:
Stadt City of Jülich

1987
Haus der Geschichte in
Bonn
Wettbewerb Competition

1987
Bibliothek der Library of
TU Berlin
Wettbewerb 4. Preis
Competition 4ᵗʰ Prize

1988
Bebauung Development
„An der Alten Kirche"
Krefeld
Städtebauliches
Gutachten Town planning
expert opinion
AG mit in collaboration with
Heinz Döhmen

1988
Glasfachschule Glass
Vocational College
Rheinbach
Wettbewerb Competition

1988
Schule School
„Volksgarten" in
Mönchengladbach
Wettbewerb Competition

1989
Museum für Glasmalerei
Museum for Painted Glass
in Linnich
Wettbewerb 1. Preis
Competition 1ˢᵗ Prize
AG mit in collaboration with
Heinz Döhmen

1989
Museum für Luft- und
Raumfahrt Aerospace
Museum München Munich
Wettbewerb Competition
mit with Stefan Polonyi

1989
Burg Bad Münstereifel
Wettbewerb Competition

1989
Begegnungsstätte
Conference Center Wülfrath
Wettbewerb 4. Preis
Competition 4ᵗʰ Prize

1989
Hotel Schloß Rheydt
Wettbewerb 2. Preis
Competition 2ⁿᵈ Prize
AG mit in collaboration with
Heinz Döhmen

1989
Fernsehmuseum TV
Museum Mainz
Wettbewerb Competition

1989
Bundesrat Parliamentary
Upper House Bonn
Wettbewerb Competition

1989
Sporthalle Arndt-
Gymnasium Sports Hall
Arndt College Krefeld
Wettbewerb 1. Preis
Competition 1ˢᵗ Prize
AG mit in collaboration with
Heinz Döhmen
Realisiert Realized 2000
Auftraggeber Client: Stadt
City of Krefeld

1990
Kreispolizeibehörde
District Police Office **Viersen**
Beauftragung
Commissioned
AG mit in collaboration with
Heinz Döhmen
Realisiert Realized **1993**
Auftraggeber Client:
Land NRW State of North
Rhine Westphalia **vertreten**
durch represented by
Staatshochbauamt State
Building Office **Krefeld**

1990
Technologiezentrum
Technology Center **Aachen**
Wettbewerb Competition
Ankauf Purchased design

1990
Wohnbebauung
Residential development
Goerdelerstraße Aachen
Wettbewerb Competition
Ankauf Purchased design

1990
Bebauung Kaiserbad-
gelände Development
Kaiserbad grounds **Aachen**
Wettbewerb 1. Preis
Competition 1ˢᵗ Prize
Auftraggeber Client: **M.+ I.**
Ceszowski, Frankfurt
Realisiert Realized **1994**
Generalunternehmer
General contractor
HOCHTIEF AG, Aachen

1991
Technologiezentrum
Technology Center **Hagen**
Wettbewerb Competition

1991
Synagoge und Jüdisches
Zentrum Synagogue and
Jewish Center **Aachen**
Wettbewerb 3. Preis
Competition 3ᵗᵉ Prize

1991
Justizvollzugsanstalt
Prison **Gelsenkirchen**
Wettbewerb Competition

1991
Arbeitsamt Labor Office in
Halle
Wettbewerb Competition

1992
Ausbildungshotel Trainee
hotel **Haus Crange in**
Herne
Wettbewerb Competition

1992
Städtische Gesamtschule
Municipal Comprehensive
School **Viersen**
Wettbewerb 1. Preis
Competition 1ˢᵗ Prize
AG mit in collaboration with
Heinz Döhmen

1992
Bebauung Development
Halle – Spitze
Städtebaulicher
Wettbewerb Town planning
competition
Ankauf Purchased design

1993
Universität und Bibliothek
University and Library in
Cottbus
Wettbewerb Competition
AG mit in collaboration with
architekten schröder
schulte-ladbeck
Dortmund

1993
Bibliothek Library
Osnabrück
Wettbewerb Competition

1993
Galerie Architektur und
Arbeit Gelsenkirchen
Wettbewerb Competition
AG mit in collaboration with
Michael Kaus

1993
Stadtzentrum
city center **Magdeburg**
Städtebauliches
Gutachten Town planning
expert opinion
AG mit in collaboration with
architekten schröder
schulte-ladbeck,
Dortmund

1993
Land- und Amtsgericht
Regional & District Court
Bonn
Wettbewerb Competition
AG mit in collaboration with
Andrea Wallrath, Fidelis
Weinert, Köln

1993
Bebauung Development
Grafenberger Allee
Düsseldorf
Städtebauliches
Gutachten Town planning
expert opinion
AG mit in collaboration with
Gruppe Baukunst,
Kunstakademie Düsseldorf

1994
Walramplatz in Jülich
Städtebauliches
Gutachten Town planning
expert opinion

1994
Brechtener Heide
Dortmund
Städtebaulicher
Wettbewerb Town planning
Competition
AG mit in collaboration with
architekten schröder /
schulte-ladbeck,
Dortmund

1994
Museum Simeonsstift Trier
Wettbewerb 2. Preis
Competition 2nd Prize

1995
Rathausmarkt Town Hall
market place Viersen
Städtebauliches
Gutachten Town planning
expert opinion
AG mit in collaboration with
Heinz Döhmen

1995
Wasser- und Schifffahrts-
direktion Waterways &
Shipping Directorate
Magdeburg
Wettbewerb Competition

1995
Museum Felix-Nussbaum-
Haus Felix-Nussbaum-
House Osnabrück
Wettbewerb Competition

1995
Kulturzentrum Cultural
Center „Alte Kraftpost"
Bad Pirmasens
Wettbewerb 5. Preis
Competition 5th Prize

1995
5. Gesamtschule
5th Comprehensive School
Wuppertal
Wettbewerb Competition

1995
Alte Synagoge Marburg
Old Synagogue
Gutachten 2. Rang
Expert opinion Ranked 2

1995
Centrum Meerssen / NL
Masterplan
Beauftragung
Commissioned
Auftraggeber Client:
Gemeente City of
Meerssen
Realisiert Realized
1995-1996
AG mit in collaboration with
Jo Coenen, Maastricht

ab as of 1995
Centrum Meerssen / NL
Objektplanungen
Beauftragung
Commissioned
Auftraggeber Client:
Gemeente City of
Meerssen
Woningstichting Meerssen
Optiek Mestrini, Meerssen
Projektentwickler Project
developer: 3W Vastgoed,
Maastricht / NL
Woningstichting Meerssen
Realisiert Realized
1995-2005
AG mit in collaboration with
Bureau Bouwadvies,
Maastricht / NL

1995
Wohnbebauung Residential
development Karlsplatz
Duisburg-Ruhrort
Wettbewerb 1. Preis
Competition 1st Prize
Projekt Project by der IBA
Emscher Park
Auftraggeber Client: CT
Projekt- und Bauträger-
gesellschaft
Nicht realisiert Not realized

1996
Bebauung Development
Hans-Böckler-Straße
Düsseldorf
Gutachten Expert opinion
AG mit in collaboration with
Heinz Schöttli,
Schaffhausen, Ingrid van
Hüllen, Aachen

1996
„Fenster zum Park"
Wohnungen und
Kindergarten Apartments
and kindergarden in
Düsseldorf
Wettbewerb 1. Preis
Competition 1st Prize
AG mit in collaboration with
Gruppe Baukunst,
Düsseldorf

1997
Archäologisches Museum
Archeological Museum
Herne
Wettbewerb 2. Preis
Competition 2nd Prize

     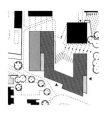

1997
Gothaer Platz in Erfurt
Wettbewerb Competition
AG mit in collaboration with
Ingrid van Hüllen

1998
Maria Montessori
Gesamtschule
Comprehensive School „Am
Moltkebahnhof" Aachen
Wettbewerb 1. Preis
Competition 1ˢᵗ Prize
Auftraggeber Client:
Stadt City of **Aachen**
Realisiert Realized **2001**
Generalplanung General
planning: **Ernst Kasper /**
Klaus Klever

2000
Kulturzentrum Cultural
Center **Paderborn**
Wettbewerb 4. Preis
Competition 4ᵗʰ Prize

2000
Justizzentrum Judicial
Center **Aachen**
Wettbewerb Competition

2000
„Casa Lupo" Malaga / SP
Beauftragt Commissioned
Auftraggeber Client:
Ehepaar Mr. & Mrs
Vonhoegen
Nicht realisiert Not realized

2001
Rathaus Town Hall **Willich**
Wettbewerb Competition

2002
Schulhaus School House
Herti in Zug / CH
Wettbewerb Competition

2002
Rathaus Bernried
Wettbewerb Competition

2002
Justizvollzugsanstalt für
weibliche Gefangene
Women's Prison **Willich**
Wettbewerb Competition

2003
Pfarrzentrum Vicarage
Bad Schussenried
Wettbewerb Competition

2003
Rathaus und Wohn-
bebauung Town Hall and
residences **Winseler / L**
Wettbewerb 2. Preis
Competition 2ⁿᵈ Prize

2003
Bebauung Development
Oosterweg in Valkenburg /
NL Städtebauliches
Gutachten Town planning
expert opinion
Auftraggeber Client: **3W**
Vastgoed, Maastricht / NL
AG mit in collaboration with
Ingrid van Hüllen

2004
Akademie Galerie
Düsseldorf
Beauftragt Commissioned
Auftraggeber Client:
Stadt City of **Düsseldorf**
AG mit in collaboration with
Dieter Willinek, Aachen
Realisiert Realized **2005**

2004
Bibliothekszentrum Library
Center **Bozen / Italien** Italy
Wettbewerb Competition
AG mit in collaboration with
Carsten Krettek

2004
Bebauung Development
„Stubengasse" Münster
Wettbewerb 1. Preis
Competition 1ˢᵗ Prize
Auftraggeber Client:
Harpen AG, Dortmund
Realisierung Realize **2006**
AG mit in collaboration with
Fritzen und Müller-
Giebeler, Ahlen

2005
Westfälisches
Landesmuseum Münster
Wettbewerb Competition
AG mit in collaboration with
Fritzen and Müller-
Giebeler, Ahlen

Ernst Kasper

1963
Diplomarbeit Ernst Kasper: „Ausbau der Burg Nideggen"
Prämiert als beste Abschlussarbeit des Jahrgangs aller Akademien und
Technischen Hochschulen der BRD (Reisestipendium)

Planungsgruppe Kasper

1979
Heizwerk und Müllverbrennungsanlage für die RWTH Aachen
Ausgezeichnet vom Land NRW als „Vorbildliches Bauwerk"

1994
Kaiserbadgelände
Mies van der Rohe Pavilion Award for European Architecture (Finalist)

1995
Deutscher Städtebaupreis (Besondere Anerkennung)

1995
Deutscher Architekturpreis (Anerkennung)

1996
West-Hyp Preis für Architektur (Besondere Anerkennung)

1996
Architekturpreis des Klempnerhandwerks (Belobigung)

1997
Deutscher Natursteinpreis (Lobende Erwähnung)

1997
BDA Preis Aachen

1998
BDA Preis Nordrhein-Westfalen

2002
Maria Montessori Gesamtschule Aachen
Gestaltungspreis der Wüstenrot Stiftung „Schulen in Deutschland –
Neubau und Revitalisierung" (1. Preisträger)

2002
2. Bundesdeutscher Architekturpreis Putz Deutscher Stuckgewerbebund
zusammen mit STO AG (Anerkennung)

2003
Auszeichnung guter Bauten 2003 des BDA Aachen

Ernst Kasper

1963
Graduation project Ernst Kasper: "Ausbau der Burg Nideggen"
Won the prize for best graduation project of the year for all acade-
mies and polytechnics in Germany (travel stipend)

Kasper Planning Group

1979
Heizwerk und Müllverbrennungsanlage für die RWTH Aachen
State of North Rhine Westphalia "Exemplary Structure" prize

1994
Kaiserbadgelände
Mies van der Rohe Pavilion Award for European Architecture
(Finalist)

1995
German Town Planning Prize (Special mention)

1995
German Architecture Prize (Distinction)

1996
West-Hyp Prize for Architecture (Special recognition)

1996
Architectural Prize awarded by the Plumbers' Association
(Special commendation)

1997
German Natural Stone Prize (Special Praise)

1997
BDA Prize, Aachen

1998
BDA Prize North Rhine-Westphalia

2002
Maria Montessori Gesamtschule Aachen
Design Prize bestowed by the Wüstenrot Foundation for "Schools in Germany
– New Buildings and Revitalization" (1st Prize)

2002
2nd Federal German Architectural Prize for Plasterwork
German Stucco Makers Associations together with STO AG
(Special Distinction)

2003
Received the BDA Aachen Good Building 2003 award

Heizwerk und Müllverbrennungsanlage
Baumeister 4/86

Berufsbildende Schulen Viersen Kempen
Baumeister 1/80
AA L' ARCHITECTURE D' AUJOURD'HUI 9/81

Sanierung Schnellengasse Eschweiler
Arch+ 7/1981
AA L' ARCHITECTURE D' AUJOURD'HUI 2/80

Gymnasium Mönchengladbach
Baumeister 1/80
Bauwelt 23/85

Ernst Kasper: „Erfahrungen und Projekte" in:
Architekturkonzepte der Gegenwart
P. Schweger (Hg), Stuttgart 1983

„Ernst Kasper" in:
monArch 1 6/88

Kulturhaus Jülich
Pesch, F.: Neues Bauen in historischer Umgebung
Rudolf Müller 1995
Bauwelt 47/92

Kaiserbadgelände
Pesch, F.: Neues Bauen in historischer Umgebung
Rudolf Müller 1995

Fundacio Mies van der Rohe, Barcelona:
Mies van der Rohe Pavilion for European Architecture 1994
Barcelona, 1995
E. Kasper, K. Klever: Das Kaiserbad, der Neubau und sein
historischer Hintergrund
Thouet Verlag, Aachen 1995
Bauwelt 10/95
wettbewerbe aktuell 4/95
a+u, architecture + urbanisme 8/95
Der Architekt 5/95
transparent Heft 4
BETON PRISMA 68/95
DBZ Deutsche Bauzeitschrift 5/96
Süddeutsche Zeitung 18./ 19. 5. 1996
Baukultur in NRW 1999

Archäologisches Museum Herne
Bauwelt 44/97

Maria Montessori Gesamtschule Aachen
Wettbewerbe aktuell 11/2002
Die Mappe 10/2002 „Polychromie einer Schule"
AIT 5/2003 „Natürlicher Bauplan"
Wüstenrot Stiftung Stuttgart: Schulen in Deutschland
Karl Krämer Verlag, Stuttgart 2004